THE SATURDAY EVENING POST
Christmas Book

THE SATURDAY EVENING POST
Christmas Book

RUSH

Norman Rockwell

THE CURTIS PUBLISHING COMPANY   INDIANAPOLIS, INDIANA

STAFF FOR THIS BOOK

Starkey Flythe, Jr., *Editor-in-Chief*
Jean White, *Text Editor*
Sandra Strother Kandrac, *Designer*
David M. Price, *Production Manager*
Jack Merritt, *Book Division Manager*
Jinny Sauer, *Assistant Designer*
Astrid Henkels and James Beaudry, *Copy Staff*
Marie Caldwell, Kay Rhea and Lynn Troup, *Compositors*
Lucian Lupinski, *Staff Artist*
Dan Shaw and Marcia Mattingly, *Art Assistants*

First Printing 1976
Second Printing 1977
Third Printing 1978
Fourth Printing 1978
Fifth Printing 1979

Now is the season of the holly and the mistletoe;
the days are come in which we hang our rooms with the sober green of December
and feel it summer in our hearts.

THE SATURDAY EVENING POST, DECEMBER 29, 1866

It is a good thing to observe Christmas day.
The mere marking of times and seasons, when men agree to stop work
and make merry together, is a wise and wholesome custom.
It helps one to feel the supremacy of the common life over the individual life.
It reminds a man to set his own little watch, now and then,
by the great clock of humanity which runs on sun time.

But there is a better thing than the observance of Christmas day,
and that is keeping Christmas.

Are you willing to forget what you have done for other people,
and to remember what other people have done for you;
to ignore what the world owes you, and to think what you owe the world;
to put your rights in the background, and your duties in the middle distance,
and your chances to do a little more than your duty in the foreground;
to see that your fellowmen are just as real as you are,
and try to look behind their faces to their hearts hungry for joy;
to own that probably the only good reason for your existence
is not what you are going to get out of life, but what you are going to give to life;
to close your book of complaints against the management of the universe,
and look around you for a place where you can sow a few seeds of happiness—
are you willing to do these things even for a day?
Then you can keep Christmas.

Are you willing to stoop down and consider the needs and the desires of little children;
to remember the weakness and loneliness of people who are growing old;
to stop asking how much your friends love you,
and ask yourself whether you love them enough;
to bear in mind the things that other people have to bear in their hearts;
to try to understand what those who live in the same house with you really want,
without waiting for them to tell you;
to trim your lamp so that it will give more light and less smoke,
and to carry it in front so that your shadow will fall behind you;
to make a grave for your ugly thoughts and a garden for your kindly feelings,
with the gate open—
are you willing to do these things even for a day?
Then you can keep Christmas.

Are you willing to believe that love is the strongest thing in the world—
stronger than hate, stronger than evil, stronger than death—
and that the blessed life which began in Bethlehem nineteen hundred years ago
is the image and brightness of the Eternal Love?
Then you can keep Christmas,

And if you can keep it for a day, why not always?
But you can never keep it alone.

HENRY VAN DYKE

Contents

Introduction

Christmas is the happiest day of the year and the shortest (almost—the actual winter solstice, when the sun reaches its greatest declination north and south, is December 21). It is such a happy day that the most popular Christmas stories are the saddest, the ones about poor little match girls in the snow or crippled children ignoring their afflictions; it is almost as though there were a conspiracy to discourage the natural ebullience of the day, the day when, since Christmas has its origins in pagan festivals, primitive man realized the world was not coming to an end, only the year, that the days would get no shorter, would indeed begin to get longer and warmer and that beneath the frozen, iron-hard earth life was stirring, bulbs swelling, sap rising and from these signs of nature, men's spirits soared.

In the celebration of a birthday we rejoice in the promise, the possibility of existence, for the little boy whose birth we mark fought against time and man's very nature to prove that the other man, the neighbor, is more valuable than the concept of good or any abstract perfection. Of himself he thought nothing; of the sick, the poor, the social outcast he thought everything, lived with them, and at the end died for them. His life was a cheerful life though, and in his teachings and example we are urged not to pull any long faces. Christmas is the essence of what he prescribes; giving, loving and pausing to reflect on the passage of time and our place in a grander scheme.

Christmas was not always December 25; early church fathers felt that the Epiphany, or the showing forth (usually commemorated January 6), was a much greater feast than Christmas and other early writers and theologians felt that, since the world was created perfect, flowers in bloom, trees in leaf, moon full, Jesus was therefore born in the spring, sometime in March when we now celebrate Easter.

It was the Roman Emperor Constantine (288-337) who is believed to have standardized the celebration of Christmas on December 25th, choosing the season of the pagan festival of the Unconquered Sun (*sol invictus*) so as to ensure peace between his political constituency and his newly found faith. In the year 330 he removed the capital of the Roman Empire to Byzantium so as to dissociate Christianity from Roman tradition. The church he founded, Hagia Sophia, may still be seen in Istanbul. It is a stupendous monument to the new religion, much of it built with remnants of pagan cults, including the columns from the temple of Diana at Ephesus where St. Paul preached. The temple was one of the wonders of the ancient world, but its columns are dwarfed by the magnificence of the new church.

Old Germanic midwinter customs have contributed to the keeping of Christmas, too, the lighting of the Yule log, the tree and decorations with evergreens. St. Francis of Assisi introduced the manger or creche with the figures of animals, shepherds and wise men adoring the newborn Christ. St. Nicholas (circa 340) was believed to visit children, admonishing them to be a credit to their parents, threatening them with empty stockings and rewarding them in good-natured reconciliation upon evidence of even mild repentance. The Dutch brought Sinter Klaas (Santa Claus) to the new world when they settled in the colony of New Amsterdam (New York). The English established the tradition of sending cards at Christmas and from all over the world, the non-Christian world included, people have contributed to the making of the most popular of festivals.

Most of these traditions remain. Above them is the spirit of peace and goodwill, the unexplained euphoria that comes upon us, Scrooge included, even against our will. We forget for a day the competition, the turmoil of day-to-day existence, and find in this moment of stock-taking that we will ever make new resolutions to improve, will fail in the larger portion, but may succeed in one or two promises and will always lose in our arguments against hope.

Christmas is the feast of children. It is their natural innocence that believes, not what adults have told them, but the evidence of their pure and unjaundiced eyes. In time, children grown old come to look on their beliefs as foolish, but in time again they look back on them as wise. Christmas urges us to believe and to make concrete our beliefs in our lives.

Starkey Flythe, Jr.

xi

THE MIRACLE

CHRISTMAS

Saint Luke

In Bethlehem

A Greek physician who learned about Jesus only after the Crucifixion, Luke was not one of the Twelve Apostles. He never even saw Jesus, so no part of his Gospel is an eyewitness account. He had, however, good sources of information. He knew well men who knew Jesus well. He heard them tell, over and over, the stories of Jesus' life and teachings, his travels, and the miracles he performed.

When Luke wrote his Gospel, probably between A.D. 60 and 70, he included many details that authors Matthew, Mark and John left out of their accounts. Interestingly, some of these details are the kind a doctor would think worth recording. For example, when Luke tells of Jesus healing a man's withered hand, he tells us it was the man's right hand. When he tells of a man "possessed of a demon" he adds a detail about the man's condition—the man had refused to wear clothing—that points clearly to mental illness.

We know that Luke was well educated, and we know that he was a sympathetic, sensitive person. He is described as a "beloved" physician, and he reappears in Acts as the trusted friend and traveling companion of Paul and Timothy. More often than the other authors of the Gospels, he mentions the emotional responses of people he writes about. For example, he mentions tears and weeping more often than the other writers.

From whom did Luke hear the story of Jesus' birth? He might have heard it from Mary herself. It is known that Mary lived on after the death of Christ, quite possibly with John in Jerusalem. Luke spent two years in Caesarea, just a few miles away, at a time when she might still have been living. It seems likely that he would have gone to visit her, and asked her to tell all she could remember of the great events that had touched her life.

However Luke learned the story, he retold it well. His account is lyrical, touched with mystery, and yet a very real story of flesh-and-blood human beings who lived in a world where there was discomfort, cold, and darkness. Luke's account of the first Christmas as it appears in the King James Version may be the best known and most loved passage in all the world's literature.

AND IT CAME TO PASS IN THOSE DAYS, THAT there went out a decree from Caesar Augustus, that all the world should be taxed.

(*And* this taxing was first made when Cyrenius was governor of Syria.)

And all went to be taxed, every one into his own city.

And Joseph also went up from Galilee, out of the city of Nazareth, into Judaea, unto the city of David, which is called Bethlehem (because he was of the house and lineage of David);

To be taxed with Mary his espoused wife, being great with child.

And so it was, that, while they were there, the days were accomplished that she should be delivered.

And she brought forth her firstborn son, and wrapped him in swaddling clothes, and laid him in a manger; because there was no room for them in the inn.

And there were in the same country shepherds abiding in the field, keeping watch over their flock by night.

And, lo, the angel of the Lord came upon them, and the glory of the Lord shone round about them; and they were sore afraid.

And the angel said unto them, Fear not: for, behold, I

2

A fifteenth-century Italian street scene circles Fra Angelico's and Fra Filippo Lippi's Adoration of the Magi. The two monks labored for five years on their masterpiece.

3

To escape the fury of King Herod, Joseph and Mary fled into Egypt, a journey (then) of some 200 miles. Herod, the lifelong friend of

bring you good tidings of great joy, which shall be to all people.

For unto you is born this day in the city of David a Saviour, which is Christ the Lord.

And this *shall* be a sign unto you: Ye shall find the babe wrapped in swaddling clothes, lying in a manger.

And suddenly there was with the angel a multitude of the heavenly host praising God, and saying,

Glory to God in the highest, and on earth peace, good will toward men.

And it came to pass, as the angels were gone away from them into heaven, the shepherds said one to another, Let us now go even unto Bethlehem, and see this thing which is come to pass, which the Lord hath made known unto us.

And they came with haste, and found Mary, and Joseph, and the babe lying in a manger.

And when they had seen *it*, they made known abroad the saying which was told them concerning this child.

And all they that heard *it* wondered at those things

Marc Antony and Caesar, was plagued in his last years by madness and the cruelty which ordered the murder of all Jewish boy babies.

which were told them by the shepherds.

But Mary kept all these things, and pondered *them* in her heart.

And the shepherds returned, glorifying and praising God for all the things that they had heard and seen, as it was told unto them.

And when eight days were accomplished for the circumcising of the child, his name was called JESUS, which was so named of the angel before he was conceived in the womb.

And when the days of her purification according to the law of Moses were accomplished, they brought him to Jerusalem, to present *him* to the Lord;

As it is written in the law of the Lord. . .

And to offer a sacrifice according to that which is said in the law of the Lord, a pair of turtledoves, or two young pigeons. . .

And when they had performed all things according to the law of the Lord, they returned into Galilee, to their own city of Nazareth.

5

Saint Matthew

The Coming of Three Kings

Matthew, who wrote this account of the Nativity, was a tax collector before he became one of the Twelve Apostles. He was at his desk in the tax office when Jesus, passing, said to him, "Follow Me," and changed his life. Why did Jesus choose a representative of the hated Roman government? Perhaps for his professional skills. A tax man would be used to keeping accurate records; and perhaps Jesus intended Matthew to make notes and record, for posterity, the story of his travels and teaching.

Matthew was not, of course, an eyewitness to the events recounted here. From whom did he hear this story? Some scholars think Matthew may have questioned Joseph and based this account on his memories of the magic night when a star stood over a stable and made Bethlehem the center of the world.

NOW THE BIRTH OF JESUS CHRIST WAS ON this wise: When as his mother Mary was espoused to Joseph, before they came together, she was found with child of the Holy Ghost.

Then Joseph her husband, being a just *man*, and not willing to make her a public example, was minded to put her away privily.

But while he thought on these things, behold, the angel of the Lord appeared unto him in a dream, saying, Joseph, thou son of David, fear not to take unto thee Mary thy wife: for that which is conceived in her is of the Holy Ghost.

And she shall bring forth a son, and thou shalt call his name JESUS: for he shall save his people from their sins.

Now all this was done, that it might be fulfilled which was spoken of the Lord by the prophet, saying,

Behold, a virgin shall be with child, and shall bring forth a son, and they shall call his name Emmanuel, which being interpreted is, God with us.

Then Joseph being raised from sleep did as the angel of the Lord had bidden him, and took unto him his wife:

And knew her not till she had brought forth her firstborn son: and he called his name JESUS.

Now when Jesus was born in Bethlehem of Judea in the days of Herod the king, behold, there came wise men from the east to Jerusalem,

Saying, Where is he that is born King of the Jews? for we have seen his star in the east, and are come to worship him.

When Herod the king had heard *these things*, he was troubled, and all Jerusalem with him.

And when he had gathered all the chief priests and scribes of the people together, he demanded of them where Christ should be born.

And they said unto him, In Bethlehem of Judaea: for thus it is written by the prophet,

And thou Bethlehem, *in* the land of Judah, art not the least among the princes of Judah: for out of thee shall come a Governor, that shall rule my people Israel.

Then Herod, when he had privily called the wise men, inquired of them diligently what time the star appeared.

And he sent them to Bethlehem, and said, Go and search diligently for the young child; and when ye have found *him*, bring me word again, that I may come and worship him also.

When they had heard the king, they departed; and, lo, the star, which they saw in the east, went before them, till it came and stood over where the young child was.

When they saw the star, they rejoiced with exceeding great joy.

And when they were come into the house, they saw the young child with Mary his mother, and fell down, and worshipped him: and when they had opened their treasures, they presented unto him gifts; gold, and frankincense, and myrrh.

And being warned of God in a dream that they should not return to Herod, they departed into their own country another way.

And when they were departed, behold, the angel of the Lord appeareth to Joseph in a dream, saying, Arise, and take the young child and his mother, and flee into Egypt, and be thou there until I bring thee word: for Herod will seek the young child to destroy him.

When he arose, he took the young child and his mother by night, and departed into Egypt.

Hieronymus Bosch's Nativity scene places Bethlehem in a cold northern landscape where shepherds warm their hands over a tiny fire.

Billy Graham

Angels

Dr. S. W. Mitchell, a celebrated Philadelphia neurologist, had gone to bed after an exceptionally tiring day. Suddenly he was awakened by someone knocking on his door. Opening it he found a little girl, poorly dressed and deeply upset. She told him her mother was very sick and asked him if he would please come with her. It was a bitterly cold, snowy night, but though he was bone tired, Dr. Mitchell dressed and followed the girl.

He found the mother desperately ill with pneumonia. After arranging for medical care, he complimented the sick woman on the intelligence and persistence of her little daughter. The woman looked at him strangely and then said, "My daughter died a month ago." She added, "Her shoes and coat are in the clothes closet there." Dr. Mitchell, amazed and perplexed, went to the closet and opened the door. There hung the very coat worn by the little girl who had brought him to tend to her mother. It was warm and dry and could not possibly have been out in the wintry night.

The Reverend John G. Paton, a missionary in the New Hebrides Islands, tells a thrilling story involving the protective care of angels. Hostile natives surrounded his mission headquarters one night, intent on burning the Patons out and killing them. John Paton and his wife prayed all during that terror-filled night that God would deliver them. When daylight came they were amazed to see the attackers unaccountably leave. They thanked God for delivering them.

A year later, the chief of the tribe was converted to Christianity, and Mr. Paton, remembering what had happened, asked the chief what had kept him and his men from burning down the house and killing them. The chief replied in surprise, "Who were all those men you had with you there?" The missionary answered, "There were no men there; just my wife and I." The chief argued that they had seen many men standing guard—hundreds of big men in shining garments with drawn swords in their hands. They seemed to circle the mission station so that the natives were afraid to attack. Only then did Mr. Paton realize that God had sent His angels to protect them. The chief agreed that there was no other explanation.

Angels announce, warn, protect. Wings symbolize their incorporeality, go back to the winged Egyptian sun god, Horus.

A north German painter used his own daughter as a model for these angels.

During World War II, Captain Eddie Rickenbacker was shot down over the Pacific Ocean. For weeks nothing was heard of him. The newspapers reported his disappearance and across the country thousands of people prayed. Mayor LaGuardia asked the whole city of New York to pray for him.

Then he returned. The Sunday papers headlined the news, and in an article, Captain Rickenbacker himself told what had happened. "And this part I would hesitate to tell," he wrote, "except that there were six witnesses who saw it with me.

"A gull came out of nowhere, and lighted on my head—I reached up my hand very gently—I killed him and then we divided him equally among us. We ate every bit, even the little bones. Nothing ever tasted so good." This gull saved the lives of Rickenbacker and his companions.

Years later I asked him to tell me the story personally, because it was through this experience that he came to know Christ. He said, "I have no explanation except that God sent one of His angels to rescue us. . . ."

Does it not seem mysterious that God brought the first message of the birth of Jesus to ordinary people rather than to princes and kings? In this instance, God spoke through His holy angel to the shepherds who were keeping sheep in the fields. This was a lowly occupation, so shepherds were not well educated. But Mary in her song, the Magnificat, tells us the true story: "He hath put down the mighty from their seats, and exalted them of low degree. He hath filled the hungry with good things, and the rich he hath sent empty away" (Luke 1:52, 53). What a word for our generation!

What was the message of the angel to the shepherds? First, he told them not to be afraid. Over and over again the presence of angels was frightening to those to whom they came. But unless they came in judgment, the angels spoke a word of reassurance. They calmed the people to whom they came. This tells us that the appearance of an angel is awe-inspiring, something about them awakening fear in the human heart. They represent a presence that has greatness and sends a chill down the spine. But when the angel had quieted the fears of the shepherds, he brought this message, one forever to be connected with the evangel:

"For behold I bring you good tidings of great joy, which shall be to all people. For unto you is born this day in the city of David a Saviour, which is Christ the Lord."

Arthur C. Clarke

What Was the Christmas Star?

Was it a comet, or two planets in conjunction? Or could it have been a blinding flash that started its trip toward the earth 3,000 years before?

Go out of doors any morning this December, an hour or so before dawn, and look up at the eastern sky. You will see there one of the most beautiful sights in all the heavens, a blazing, blue-white beacon, ten times brighter than Sirius, the most brilliant of the stars. Apart from the moon itself, it is the brightest object you will ever see in the night sky. It will still be visible even when the sun rises; indeed, you can find it at midday if you know exactly where to look.

Ours is an age in which the glare of electric lights has hidden the stars, so that men have forgotten many things that were familiar to their ancestors. If you take the average city dweller away from his floodlit canyons, lead him out to some hill in the country, and show him this brilliant herald of the dawn, he probably will have no idea what it is. Indeed, it is safe to predict that through December there will be a flood of flying-saucer reports from ignorant or credulous observers seeing this dazzling point of light against the sunrise.

It is our sister world, the planet Venus, reflecting across the gulf of space the sunlight glancing from her unbroken cloud veils. Every eighteen months she appears in the morning sky, rising shortly before the sun.

It has been seriously suggested that Venus was the Star of Nativity, and at least one massive book has been written in an effort to prove this theory. However, it is a theory that makes very little sense when examined closely. To all the peoples of the Eastern world, Venus was one of the most familiar objects in the sky. Even today, she serves as a kind of alarm clock to the Arab nomads. When she rises, it is time to start moving, to make as much progress as possible before the sun begins to blast the desert with its heat. For thousands of years, shining more brilliantly than we ever see her in our northern skies, she has watched the camps struck and the caravans begin to move.

Even to uneducated Jews, there could have been nothing in the least remarkable about Venus. And the Magi were no ordinary men; they were certainly experts on astronomy, and knew the movements of the planets.

What, then, was the Star of Bethlehem—assuming that it was a natural phenomenon and not a miraculous apparition? The Bible gives us very few clues; all we can do is consider some possibilities that at this distance in time can be neither proved nor disproved. One of those possibilities—the most spectacular and awe-inspiring of all—has been suggested only in the past few years. But let us first look at some of the earlier theories.

In addition to Venus there are four other planets easily visible to the naked eye—Mercury, Mars, Jupiter and Saturn. During their movements across the sky, two planets may sometimes appear to pass very close to one another, though in fact they are millions or hundreds of millions of miles apart. Such occurrences are called "conjunctions."

On very rare occasions, the conjunctions may be so close that the planets cannot be separated by the naked eye. This happened to Mars and Venus on October 4, 1953, when for a short while the two planets appeared to be fused into a single star. Such a spectacle is rare enough to be very striking, and the great astronomer Kepler devoted much time to proving that the Star of Bethlehem was a conjunction of Jupiter and Saturn. The two planets passed very close together (remember, this was purely from Earth's point of view—in reality they were half a billion miles apart!) in May, 7 B.C., not long before the date set by some authorities for the birth of Christ. Others set it as late as 4 B.C.

Kepler's ingenious proposal, however, is as unconvincing as the Venus theory. Better calculations than he could make in his day have shown that, after all, this conjunction was not a very close one, and the planets were always far enough apart to be separated easily by the eye. Moreover, there was a still closer conjunction in 66 B.C., which, following Kepler's theory, should have brought a delegation of wise men to Bethlehem fifty-nine years too soon!

In any case, the Magi could be expected to be as familiar with such events as with all other planetary movements, and the Biblical account also indicates that the Star of Bethlehem was visible over a period of weeks (it must have taken the Magi a considerable time to reach Judea, have their interview with Herod and then go on to Bethlehem). The conjunction of two planets lasts only a few hours, since they soon separate in the sky and go on their individual ways again.

We can get around this difficulty if we assume that the Magi were astrologers and had somehow deduced the birth of the Messiah from a particular configuration of the heavens. Suppose, for example, they had decided, by some esoteric reasoning of the type on which this pseudo science is based, that Venus or some other planet, perhaps Jupiter or Saturn, had taken a position in the Zodiac that foretold the birth of Christ. Then even when the planet concerned moved from this position, they might still refer to it as "His" star and continue to use it as a guide.

This theory is simple and plausible, for in ancient times most wise men did believe in astrology and, in consequence, many of them led somewhat precarious lives as court prophets. Because of its very simplicity, this theory can never be proved or disproved, but one would like to think that the facts are somewhat more exciting.

They may well be. It seems much more likely that the Star of the Nativity was something quite novel and unusual, and not one of the familiar planets whose behavior had been well known for thousands of years before the birth of Christ. Of course, if one accepts as literally true the statement that "the star, which they saw in the east, *went before them, till it came and stood over where the young Child was,*" no natural explanation is possible. Any heavenly body—star, planet, comet or whatever it may be—must share in the normal movement of the sky, rising in the east and setting some hours later in the west. Only the Pole Star, because it lies on the invisible axis of the turning Earth, appears unmoving in the sky and can act as a fixed and constant guide.

But the phrase "went before them," like so much else in the Bible, can be interpreted in many ways. It may be that the Star, whatever it might have been, was so close to the Sun that it could only be seen for a short period near dawn, and so would never have been visible except in the eastern sky. Like Venus when she is a morning star, it might have risen shortly before the Sun, then been lost in the glare of the new day before it could climb very far up the sky. The wise men would thus have seen it ahead of them at the beginning of each day, and then lost it in the dawn before it had veered round to the south. Many other readings are equally possible.

Very well then, can we discover some astronomical phenomenon that fits the Biblical text and is sufficiently startling to surprise men completely familiar with the movements of the stars and planets?

Let's see if a comet answers the specification. Most comets have a bright, starlike core or nucleus that is completely dwarfed by an enormous tail, a luminous appendage which may be in the shape of a narrow beam or a broad, diffuse fan. At first sight it would seem very unlikely that anyone would call such an object a star, but in old records comets are sometimes referred to, not inaptly, as "hairy stars."

It is perfectly possible that a comet appeared just before the birth of Christ. Attempts have been made, without success, to discover whether any of the known comets were visible around that date. But the number of comets whose paths and periods we do know is very small compared with the colossal number that undoubtedly exists. If a comet did shine over Bethlehem, it may not be seen again from Earth for a hundred thousand years.

We can picture it in that Oriental dawn, a band of light streaming up from the eastern horizon, perhaps stretching vertically toward the zenith. The tail of a comet always points away from the sun; the comet would appear, therefore, like a great arrow, aimed at the east. As the sun rose, the comet would fade into invisibility; but the next morning, it would be in almost the same place, still directing the travelers to their goal. It might be visible for weeks before it disappeared once more into the depths of space. The picture is a dramatic and attractive one. It may even be the correct explanation; one day, perhaps, we shall know.

But there is another theory, and this is the one most astronomers would probably accept today. It makes the

The great Post artist, J.C. Leyendecker, portrays a wimpled medieval Lady Bountiful making her rounds with page, mistletoe and gifts.

other explanations look trivial and commonplace indeed, for it leads us to contemplate the most astonishing and terrifying events yet discovered in the whole realm of Nature.

We will forget now about planets and comets and the other denizens of our own tight little solar system. Let us go out across *real* space, right out to the stars—those other suns, many of them far greater than our own sun.

Most stars shine with unwavering brilliance, century after century. Sirius appears now exactly as it did to Moses, as it did to Neanderthal Man, as it did to the dinosaurs, if they ever bothered to look at the night sky. Its brilliance has changed little during the entire history of Earth, and will be the same a billion years from now.

The Wise Men may have come from Alexandria.

But there are some stars, the so-called "novae" or new stars, that for no ascertainable reason suddenly turn themselves into celestial atomic bombs. Such a star may explode so violently that it leaps a hundred-thousand-fold in brilliance within a few hours. One night it may be invisible to the naked eye; on the next, it may dominate the sky.

Novae are not uncommon; many are observed every year, though few are near enough to be visible except through telescopes. They are the routine disasters of the universe.

Two or three times in every thousand years, however, there occurs something that makes a mere nova about as inconspicuous as a firefly at noon. When a star becomes a *super*nova its brilliance may increase not by a hundred thousand but by a *thousand million* times in the course of a few hours. The last time such an event was witnessed was in A.D. 1604; there was another supernova in A.D. 1572 (so brilliant that it was visible in broad daylight);

and the Chinese astronomers recorded one in A.D. 1054. It is quite possible that the Star of Bethlehem was such a supernova, and if so one can draw some very surprising conclusions.

We'll assume that Supernova Bethlehem was about as bright as the nova of A.D. 1572, often called Tycho's star after the great astronomer who observed it at the time. Since this star could be seen by day, it must have been as brilliant as Venus. As we also know that a supernova is, in reality, at least a hundred million times more brilliant than our own sun, a simple calculation tells us how far away it must have been for its *apparent* brightness to equal that of Venus.

The calculation shows that Supernova Bethlehem was more than 3,000 light-years or, if you prefer, 18,000,000,000,000,000 miles away. That means its light had been traveling for at least three thousand years before it reached Earth and Bethlehem, so that the awesome cataclysm of which it was the evidence really took place five thousand years ago, when the great Pyramid was still fresh from the builders.

Let us, in imagination, cross the gulfs of space and time and go back to the moment of the catastrophe. We might find ourselves watching an ordinary star—a sun perhaps no different from our own. There may have been planets circling it; we do not know how common planets are in the Universe nor how many suns have such small companions. But there is no reason to think they are rare, and many novae must be the funeral pyres of worlds, and perhaps races, greater than ours.

There is no warning at all, only a steadily rising intensity of the sun's light. Within minutes the change is noticeable: within an hour, the nearer worlds are burning. The star is expanding like a balloon, blasting off shells of gas at a million miles an hour as it blows its outer layers into space. Within a day, it is shining with such supernal brilliance that it gives off more light than *all the other suns in the universe combined.* If it had planets, they are now no more than flecks of flame in the still expanding shells of fire. The conflagration will burn for weeks before the dying star collapses into quiescence.

But let us consider what happens to the light of the nova, which moves a hundred times more swiftly than the blast wave of the explosion. It will spread out into space, and after four or five years it will reach the next star. If there are planets circling that star, they will suddenly be illuminated by a second sun. It will give them no appreciable heat, but will be bright enough to banish night completely, for it will be more than a thousand times more luminous than our full moon. All that light will come from a single blazing point, since even from its nearest neighbor Supernova Bethlehem would appear too small to show a disc.

To the lowly shepherds, the star brought hope.

Century after century, the shell of light will continue to expand around its source. It will flash past countless suns and flare briefly in the skies of their planets. Indeed, by the most conservative estimate, this great new star must have shone over thousands of worlds before its light reached Earth, and to all those worlds it appeared far, far brighter than it did to the men it led to Judea.

For as the shell of light expanded, it faded also. By the time it reached Bethlehem it was spread over the surface of a sphere six thousand light-years across. A thousand years earlier, when Homer sang of Troy, the nova would have appeared twice as brilliant to any watchers farther upstream, as it were, closer to the time and place of the explosion.

That is a strange thought: there is a stranger one to come. For the light of Supernova Bethlehem is still flooding out through space. It has left Earth far behind in the twenty centuries that have elapsed since men saw it for the first and last time. Now its light is spread over a sphere ten thousand light-years across, and must be correspondingly fainter. It is simple to calculate how bright the Supernova must be to any beings who may be seeing it now as a new star in *their* skies. To them, it will still be far more brilliant than any other star in their entire heavens, for its brightness will have decreased only by 50 percent on its extra two thousand years of travel. . . .

At this very moment, therefore, the Star of Bethlehem may still be shining in the skies of countless worlds, circling far suns. Any watchers on those worlds will see its sudden appearance and its slow fading, just as the Magi may have seen it two thousand years ago when the expanding shell of light swept past Earth. And for thousands of years to come, as its radiance ebbs out toward the frontiers of the universe, Supernova Bethlehem will still have power to startle all who see it, wherever and *what*ever they may be.

Astronomy, as nothing else can do, teaches men humility. We know now that our sun is merely one undistinguished member of a vast family of stars, and no longer think of ourselves as being at the center of Creation. Yet it is strange to think that before its light fades away below the limits of vision, we may have shared the Star of Bethlehem with the beings of perhaps a million worlds, and that to many of them, nearer to the source of the explosion, it must have been a far more wonderful sight than ever it was to human eyes. What did they make of it, and did it bring them good tidings, or ill?

Donald Culross Peattie

Winter Wonder

When the skies are lowest, when the gray clouds hang heavy with a great stillness and the winter-locked world lies waiting for some reprieve from despair, then falls the miracle of snow. It falls like a blessing, softly, silently, making a white beauty where outlines were bleak and colors were dun. As it veils the stone and smut of the cities, or draws its gentle blanket over fences and frozen ruts in the country byways, we too know its softening influence; men go walking with faces uplifted to feel that feathery cold touch.

The air is filled with a numberless whiteness. Some purity is abroad that is not of this earth. And if you pause and examine some of those first, great flakes lying unmelted on your coat sleeve, you will see the most delicate and fleeting perfection that Nature ever creates.

For it is in such an hour, when clouds are low, humidity is great, and the air is still, that the finest of snowflakes are formed and reach us in their most flawless perfection.

Snow covers the defects of a man-scarred world.

Most of the snow in the world never descends to us. Vast quantities of it are created in lofty clouds even in warm latitudes, but it melts as it falls through the warmer air, and reaches us as rain. In the icy north, of course, snow is a frequent visitant, but in that dry and frosty air it does not attain the marvelous gemlike size and pattern you find in a damp snowstorm in a milder climate, but whirls along in tiny icy pellets driven by whiplike winds.

So it is in our temperate climate that winter makes its finest display. One snowstorm, and the sad and bad old world we know so well has turned a new page. All is fair and new and pure, waiting to be inscribed. The least step of a sparrow may be noted there, and the footprints of the deer mice, with the dragging tail mark between; you can see the very leap of a cottontail in the spacing of his pad prints on the white sheet.

Now all our trees come into new unearthly bloom; old scars are hidden, and cleanliness lies like healing over all. That it is transient makes it no less dear. It will grow old and gray and tiresome, like man himself. But the first snowstorm, even more, the first flakes of that first snow, are perfect as only the newborn are perfect, and bring with them that same innocent air of being messengers from heaven.

A snowflake, of course, is simply the water vapor in the air crystallized into a geometrical shape. Simply, I say—yet the bewildering multiplicity of forms which a snowflake may take is beyond the power of the most accomplished worker in metal or wood or stone.

Hundreds and hundreds of patterns have been recorded, endlessly varying in detail. But every one is built upon the same principle, the hexagonal or six-faced crystal, and every last complexity of its design may be divided by six or three.

The reason for this is fundamental. Water, as we learned in school, is composed of two gases—hydrogen and oxygen—in the proportion of two parts hydrogen to one part oxygen; its nuclear atoms are so arranged as to produce each crystalline structure on a triangular basis. Nothing in nature is lovelier, and nothing in art has been more enduring, than this simple plan, with the connotation of holiness which the trinity brings to mind.

And snowflakes, of all things, are most truly made in heaven. They crystallize while floating about in the air, so that the atoms and molecules, which are the building blocks of all things, have a unique freedom in which to arrange themselves. As they descend through varying strata of moisture and temperature and air current, they grow and change and take on variety, until their intricate

16

As it falls, snow lifts spirits who hear its silence and know a peace which passeth human understanding.

DRAWN BY
SARAH S. STILWELL WEBER

elaboration surpasses anything that comes from the fingers of the most skilled lacemaker of Europe.

What a fairylike business the study of snowflakes would seem! Yet it is a respected science, with a long history. Away back in 1555, Olaus Magnus, the brother of the Archbishop of Uppsala, published in Rome à book about natural curiosities. That book contains what seems to be the first published drawing of a snowflake. It is a crude woodcut, and but for the legend beneath it might be mistaken for some other of Olaus' collection of curiosa. But it reminds us, at least, how long men have looked up and wondered at this gift from the skies.

In 1820 the arctic explorer, William Scoresby, recorded in a superb collection of drawings a variety of flake patterns. But drawing is a slow and inexact method of reproducing their passing wonder.

It has remained for the modern method of microscopic photography to catch this accurately, and one enthusiast in particular, W.A. Bentley of Vermont, has spent a lifetime in pursuit of the snowflake. Even the X ray has been turned upon it, to learn the last secrets of its structure.

For most of us it is enough to take the snowflake for its sheer delight, or, if you want to dig philosophy out of it, for testimony that in nature, at least, there is sound organization down to the last and most delicate detail.

When the clouds have emptied their bag of goose-feather whiteness, it is the wind that takes a hand at making over the world.

Never was stuff so malleable as snow, so easy and quick to work, and never was artist so free as the wind.

Now over the last year's nest is cocked a peaked new roof, now every fence post is capped, and the baldest ditch is softened to a slope like the flank of some great crouching beast.

The very currents of the wind that helped to shape the flake are written, with the tracks of wildlife, on the fields of white. And tomorrow, if the wind blows all night long and more snow falls, the careless sculptor will have shaped the world all over again.

Snow, in this soft blanket form, is a kindly thing. Cold as it is, it forms a shelter for little creatures crouching in its lee; it conserves earth's banked warmth, and thus protects plant life as well.

The winter form of rainfall, it provides drink for birds and animals, and is a store, indeed, of water for future irrigation, when thaws unlock it.

But snow is a force, as well, and all that soft and comfortable kindliness can turn to cruel power.

Let it freeze in a hard crust, and groundlings like quail and mice and partridge may be imprisoned under it and starve to death. Or let rain turn that snow upon the boughs to ice, and the grandest old limbs may crack and break beneath the strain. Or sudden thaw after great snowfall can end in disastrous flood.

But these are what insurance policies carefully call "an act of God." More certain are the joys of winter, the sparkle and the crunch of snow beneath the heel, the tingle at the bottom of one's lungs and the sense of blood running warmer for the cold of air.

Now skiers find their wings again; now on the front lawn rises that art form surely older than the Parthe-

The young see no colds or flu
in the magic drifts of crystal,
only the ecstasy of wind speed
and bell sounds, the rapture of
snowball-induced flying top hats.

JOHN FALTER

Kids make angels in the whiteness that reflects their innocence, hoping to puzzle adults who come later, upright or in other postures.

non—the snow man, complete with pipe and lumps of coal for eyes. Now winter berries stand out red against the white, and birds are plain to see, and sunrise or sundown glow rose-colored, with shadows that are purple-blue. The feeding tray, these days, shows us who are our true friends—cardinal and jay, and chickadee, who, by his upside-down hilarity, demonstrates that he loves winter best of all.

Nights are deeply silent, unless the owl goes hunting. Days have a bite like that you'll get when you set your teeth in a winy apple. The sun is welcome as at no other time, and finds a million diamonds to dance on, and at night the stars step forth with a grandeur and brilliance unknown to summer's skies.

The first of winter comes to us as welcome as the first of spring, all fresh and full of sparkle. Indeed it is spring that it is hiding underneath that coverlet of snow.

Next year's bloom, the waterfalls that will refresh parched August, all our eagerness for April, are to be fed by these first snowflakes twirling down, gathering, crowding, whitening the gray sky, filling our eyes and mind with the sense of a marvelous richness.

Even folks who "dread the winter"
will still hanker for "a little snow on Christmas Eve."
And in those parts of the world, including much of our own Southland,
where snow seldom falls, people take the symbol of "white Christmas"
to their hearts and pay no attention
to their climate in selecting winter-wonderland Christmas cards.
Indeed, it is not irreverent to believe that the Little Boy, whose birthday we celebrate—
who never slid down a hill in Nazareth or made a Santa Claus snowman—
may give a special meaning and promise in sometimes covering the scars
of our sad old world with a white Christmas.

THE SATURDAY EVENING POST DECEMBER 27, 1958

In our hearts it is to the deep country we return in December even though we may have been born in the city.

23

What They Said About Christmas

My best of wishes for your merry Christmases and your happy New Years, your long lives and your true prosperities. Worth twenty pound good if they are delivered as I send them. Remember? Here's a final prescription added, "To be taken for life."

—*Charles Dickens*, "Dr. Marigold's Prescriptions"

Heigh ho! sing heigh ho! unto the green holly
Most friendship is feigning, most loving mere folly.
   Then heigh ho, the holly!
   This life is most jolly!

—*William Shakespeare*

It is good to be children sometimes, and never better than at Christmas, when its mighty Founder was a child Himself.

—*Charles Dickens*

Christmas is coming, the geese are getting fat,
Please to put a penny in the old man's hat;
If you haven't got a penny, a ha'penny will do,
If you haven't got a ha'penny, God bless you!

—*Beggar's rhyme, anonymous*

Are you going to send a flaming red necktie to a quiet man with pepper-and-salt taste in clothing? Are you going to give teaspoons to a woman who already has several unused pounds of them? Are you planning to give a set of Scott's novels to a man who already has every volume? Are you planning to give large objects to people who live in small rooms? Are you going to send a potted fern to a lady who lives near the woods? Are you planning to send a dyed goatskin to a hunter? Are you forgetting that an author will already have plenty of inkwells?

"God tells us to forgive our enemies," cried the fiercest of all the Medicis, "But nowhere does He tell us to forgive our friends!" And one may well suspect that he was moved to this exasperatory burst by the receipt of an ill-chosen gift for which he was expected to be thankful.

—The Saturday Evening Post, *December 21, 1907*

Loving Father, help us remember the birth of Jesus, that we may share in the song of the angels, the gladness of the shepherds, and the worship of the wise men.

Close the door of hate and open the door of love all over the world.

Let kindness come with every gift and good desires with every greeting.

Deliver us from evil by the blessing which Christ brings, and teach us to be merry with clear hearts.

May the Christmas morning make us happy to be Thy children, and the Christmas evening bring us to our beds with grateful thoughts, forgiving and forgiven, for Jesus' sake. Amen!

—*Robert Louis Stevenson*

At Christmas I no more desire a rose
Than wish a snow in May's newfangled mirth;
But like of each thing that in season grows.

—*William Shakespeare*, Love's Labour's Lost

And so, at this Christmas time, I greet you. Not quite as the world sends greetings, but with profound esteem and with the prayer that for you, now and forever, the day breaks and the shadows flee away.

—*Fra Giovanni*

England was merry England, when
Old Christmas brought his sports again,
'Twas Christmas broach'd the mightiest ale:
'Twas Christmas told the merriest tale;
A Christmas gambol oft could cheer
The poor man's heart through half the year.

—*Sir Walter Scott*, "Lochinvar"

One Christmas was so much like another, in those years around the seatown corner now and out of all sound except the distant speaking of the voices I sometimes hear a moment before sleep, that I can never remember whether it snowed for six days and six nights when I was twelve or whether it snowed for twelve days and twelve nights when I was six.

—*Dylan Thomas*, "A Child's Christmas in Wales"

STORIES

Charles Dickens

A Christmas Carol

Marley was dead, to begin with. There is no doubt whatever about that. The register of his burial was signed by the clergyman, the clerk, the undertaker, and the chief mourner. Scrooge signed it. And Scrooge's name was good upon 'Change for anything he chose to put his hand to.

Old Marley was as dead as a doornail.

Scrooge knew he was dead? Of course he did. How could it be otherwise? Scrooge and he were partners for I don't know how many years. Scrooge was his sole executor, his sole administrator, his sole assign, his sole residuary legatee, his sole friend, his sole mourner.

Scrooge never painted out old Marley's name, however. There it yet stood, years afterwards, above the warehouse door—Scrooge and Marley. The firm was known as Scrooge and Marley. Sometimes people new to the business called Scrooge Scrooge, and sometimes Marley. He answered to both names. It was all the same to him.

Oh! But he was a tightfisted hand at the grindstone, was Scrooge! a squeezing, wrenching, grasping, scraping, clutching, covetous old sinner! External heat and cold had little influence on him. No warmth could warm, no cold could chill him. No wind that blew was bitterer than he, no falling snow was more intent upon its purpose, no pelting rain less open to entreaty. Foul weather didn't know where to have him. The heaviest rain and snow and hail and sleet could boast of the advantage over him in only one respect—they often "came down" handsomely, and Scrooge never did.

Nobody ever stopped him in the street to say, with gladsome looks, "My dear Scrooge, how are you? When will you come to see me?" No beggars implored him to bestow a trifle, no children asked him what it was o'clock, no man or woman ever once in all his life inquired the way to such and such a place, of Scrooge. Even the blind men's dogs appeared to know him, and when they saw him coming on, would tug their owners into doorways and up courts; and then would wag their tails as though they said, "No eyes at all is better than an evil eye, dark master!"

But what did Scrooge care! It was the very thing he liked. To edge his way along the crowded paths of life, warning all human sympathy to keep its distance, was what the knowing ones call "nuts" to Scrooge.

Once upon a time—of all the good days in the year, upon a Christmas eve—old Scrooge sat busy in his countinghouse. It was cold, bleak, biting, foggy weather; and the city clocks had only just gone three, but it was quite dark already.

The door of Scrooge's countinghouse was open, that he might keep his eye upon his clerk, who, in a dismal little cell beyond, a sort of tank, was copying letters. Scrooge had a very small fire, but the clerk's fire was so very much smaller that it looked like one coal. But he couldn't replenish it, for Scrooge kept the coal-box in his own room; and so surely as the clerk came in with the shovel, the master predicted that it would be necessary for them to part. Wherefore the clerk put on his white comforter, and tried to warm himself at the candle; in which effort, not being a man of a strong imagination, he failed.

"A Merry Christmas, uncle! God save you!" cried a cheerful voice. It was the voice of Scrooge's nephew, who came upon him so quickly that this was the first intimation Scrooge had of his approach.

"Bah!" said Scrooge; "humbug!"

"Christmas a humbug, uncle! You don't mean that, I am sure?"

"I do. Out upon merry Christmas! What's Christmastime to you but a time for paying bills without money; a time for finding yourself a year older, and not an hour richer; a time for balancing your books and having every item in 'em through a round dozen of months presented dead against you? If I had my will, every idiot who goes about with 'Merry Christmas' on his lips should be boiled with his own pudding, and buried with a stake of holly through his heart. He should!"

"Uncle!"

"Nephew, keep Christmas in your own way, and let me keep it in mine."

"Keep it! But you don't keep it."

"Let me leave it alone, then. Much good may it do you! Much good it has ever done you!"

Scrooge had drawn in upon himself until the mirror of his soul remarked no breath to indicate life. His coffers swelled; his heart shrank. Love, Christmas, friends—fixed stars in the gray guarantee of existence—were dark voids to him.

"There are many things from which I might have derived good, by which I have not profited, I dare say, Christmas among the rest. But I am sure I have always thought of Christmastime, when it has come round—apart from the veneration due to its sacred origin, if anything belonging to it can be apart from that—as a good time; a kind, forgiving, charitable, pleasant time; the only time I know of, in the long calendar of the year, when men and women seem by one consent to open their shut-up hearts freely, and to think of people below them as if they really were fellow-travellers to the grave, and not another race of creatures bound on other journeys. And therefore, uncle, though it has never put a scrap of gold or silver in my pocket, I believe that it *has* done me good, and *will* do me good; and I say, God bless it!"

The clerk in the tank involuntarily applauded.

"Let me hear another sound from you," said Scrooge, "and you'll keep your Christmas by losing your situation! You're quite a powerful speaker, sir," he added, turning to his nephew. "I wonder you don't go into Parliament."

"Don't be angry, uncle. Come! Dine with us tomorrow."

Scrooge said that he would see him—yes, indeed he did. He went the whole length of the expression, and said that he would see him in that extremity first.

"But why?" cried Scrooge's nephew. "Why?"

"Why did you get married?"

"Because I fell in love."

"Because you fell in love!" growled Scrooge, as if that were the only one thing in the world more ridiculous than a merry Christmas. "Good afternoon!"

"Nay, uncle, but you never came to see me before that

29

happened. Why give it as a reason for not coming now?"

"Good afternoon."

"I want nothing from you; I ask nothing of you; why cannot we be friends?"

"Good afternoon."

"I am sorry, with all my heart, to find you so resolute. We have never had any quarrel, to which I have been a party. But I have made the trial in homage to Christmas, and I'll keep my Christmas humour to the last. So a Merry Christmas, uncle!"

"Good afternoon!"

"And a Happy New Year!"

"Good afternoon!"

His nephew left the room without an angry word, notwithstanding.

At length the hour of shutting up arrived, and

"...not well dressed; their shoes were far from waterproof."

Scrooge, dismounting from his stool, tacitly admitted the fact to the expectant clerk in the tank, who instantly snuffed his candle out, and put on his hat.

"You want all day tomorrow, I suppose?"

"If quite convenient, sir."

"It's not convenient, and it's not fair. If I was to stop half a crown for it, you'd think yourself mightily ill used, I'll be bound?"

"Yes, sir."

"And yet you don't think me ill used, when I pay a day's wages for no work."

"It's only once a year, sir."

"A poor excuse for picking a man's pocket every twenty-fifth of December! But I suppose you must have the whole day. Be here all the earlier next morning."

The clerk promised that he would, and Scrooge walk-

ed out with a growl. The office was closed in a twinkling, and the clerk, with the long ends of his white comforter dangling below his waist (for he boasted no greatcoat), went down a slide, at the end of a lane of boys, twenty times, in honour of its being Christmas eve, and then ran home as hard as he could pelt, to play at blindman's buff.

Scrooge took his melancholy dinner in his usual melancholy tavern; and having read all the newspapers, and beguiled the rest of the evening with his banker's book, went home to bed. He lived in chambers which had once belonged to his deceased partner. They were a gloomy suite of rooms, in a lowering pile of building up a yard. The building was old enough now, and dreary enough for nobody lived in it but Scrooge, the other rooms being all let out as offices.

Now it is a fact that there was nothing at all particular about the knocker on the door of this house, except that it was very large; also, that Scrooge had seen it, night and morning, during his whole residence in that place; also, that Scrooge had as little of what is called fancy about him as any man in the city of London. And yet Scrooge, having his key in the lock of the door, saw in the knocker, without its undergoing any intermediate process of change, not a knocker, but Marley's face.

Marley's face, with a dismal light about it, like a bad lobster in a dark cellar. It was not angry or ferocious, but it looked at Scrooge as Marley used to look—ghostly spectacles turned up upon its ghostly forehead.

As Scrooge looked fixedly at this phenomenon, it was

a knocker again. He said, "Pooh, pooh!" and closed the door with a bang.

The sound resounded through the house like thunder. Every room above, and every cask in the wine merchant's cellars below, appeared to have a separate peal of echoes of its own. Scrooge was not a man to be frightened by echoes. He fastened the door, and walked across the hall, and up the stairs. Slowly too, trimming his candle as he went.

Up Scrooge went, not caring a button for its being very dark. Darkness is cheap, and Scrooge liked it. But before he shut his heavy door, he walked through his rooms to see that all was right. He had just enough recollection of Marley's ghostly face to desire to do that.

We hear the great glad tidings, the sounds of Christmas.

the room, and communicated, for some purpose now forgotten, with a chamber in the highest story of the building. It was with great astonishment, and with a strange, inexplicable dread, that, as he looked, he saw this bell begin to swing. Soon it rang out loudly, and so did every bell in the house.

This was succeeded by a clanking noise, deep down below as if some person were dragging a heavy chain over the casks in the wine merchant's cellar.

Then he heard the noise much louder, on the floors below; then coming up the stairs; then coming straight toward his door.

It came on through the heavy door, and a spectre passed into the room before him. The dying flame leaped up, as though it cried, "I know him! Marley's ghost!"

Sitting room, bedroom, lumber room, all as they should be. Nobody under the table, nobody under the sofa; a small fire in the grate; spoon and basin ready; and the little saucepan of gruel (Scrooge had a cold in his head) upon the hob. Nobody under the bed; nobody in the closet; nobody in his dressing gown, which was hanging up in a suspicious attitude against the wall. Lumber room as usual. Old fireguards, old shoes, two fish baskets, washing stand on three legs, and a poker.

Quite satisfied, he closed his door and locked himself in; double-locked himself in, which was not his custom. Thus secured against surprise, he took off his cravat, put on his dressing gown and slippers and his nightcap, and sat down before the very low fire to take his gruel.

As he threw his head back in the chair, his glance happened to rest upon a bell, a disused bell, that hung in

The same face, the very same. Marley in his pigtail, usual waistcoat, tights, and boots. His body was transparent; so that Scrooge, observing him, and looking through his waistcoat, could see the two buttons on his coat behind.

Scrooge had often heard it said that Marley had no bowels, but he had never believed it until now.

No, nor did he believe it even now. Though he looked the phantom through and through, and saw it standing before him—though he felt the chilling influence of its death-cold eyes, and noticed the very texture of the folded kerchief bound about its head and chin—he was still incredulous.

"How now!" said Scrooge, caustic and cold as ever. "What do you want with me?"

"Much!"—Marley's voice, no doubt about it.

"Who are you?"

"Ask me who I *was*."

"Who *were* you then?"

"In life I was your partner, Jacob Marley."

"Can you—can you sit down?"

"I can."

"Do it, then."

Scrooge asked the question, because he didn't know whether a ghost so transparent might find himself in a condition to take a chair; and felt that, in the event of its being impossible, it might involve the necessity of an embarrassing explanation. But the ghost sat down on the opposite side of the fireplace, as if he were quite used to sitting there.

"You don't believe in me."

"I don't."

"What evidence would you have of my reality beyond that of your senses?"

"I don't know."

"Why do you doubt your senses?"

"Because a little thing affects them. A slight disorder of the stomach makes them cheats. You may be an undigested bit of beef, a blot of mustard, a crumb of cheese, a fragment of an underdone potato. There's more of gravy than of grave about you, whatever you are!"

Scrooge was not much in the habit of cracking jokes, nor did he feel in his heart by any means waggish then. The truth is that he tried to be smart, as a means of distracting his own attention, and keeping down his horror.

But how much greater was his horror when, the phantom taking off the bandage round its head, as if it were too warm to wear indoors, its lower jaw dropped down upon its breast!

"Mercy! Dreadful apparition, why do you trouble me? Why do spirits walk the earth, and why do they come to me?"

"It is required of every man that the spirit within him should walk abroad among his fellow men, and travel far and wide; and if that spirit goes not forth in life, it is condemned to do so after death. I cannot tell you all I would. A very little more is permitted to me. I cannot rest, I cannot stay, I cannot linger anywhere. My spirit never walked beyond our countinghouse—mark me!—in life my spirit never roved beyond the narrow limits of our money-changing hole; and weary journeys lie before me!"

"Seven years dead. And travelling all the time? You travel fast?"

"On the wings of the wind."

"You might have got over a great quantity of ground in seven years."

"O blind man, blind man! not to know that ages of incessant labour by immortal creatures for this earth must pass into eternity before the good of which it is susceptible is all developed. Not to know that any Christian spirit working kindly in its little sphere, whatever it may be, will find its mortal life too short for its vast means of usefulness. Not to know that no space of regret can make amends for one life's opportunities misused! Yet I was like this man; I once was like this man!"

"But you were always a good man of business, Jacob," faltered Scrooge, who now began to apply this to himself.

"Business!" cried the Ghost, wringing its hands again. "Mankind was my business. The common welfare was my business; charity, mercy, forbearance, benevolence, were all my business. The dealings of my trade were but a drop of water in the comprehensive ocean of my business!"

Scrooge was very much dismayed to hear the spectre going on at this rate, and began to quake exceedingly.

"Hear me! My time is nearly gone."

"I will. But don't be hard upon me! Don't be flowery, Jacob! Pray!"

"I am here tonight to warn you that you have yet a chance and hope of escaping my fate. A chance and hope of my procuring, Ebenezer."

"You were always a good friend to me. Thank'ee!"

"You will be haunted by Three Spirits."

"Is that the chance and hope you mentioned, Jacob? I—I think I'd rather not."

"It is required of every man that the spirit within him should walk abroad among his fellow men, if not in life then after death."

"Without their visits, you cannot hope to shun the path I tread. Expect the first tomorrow night, when the bell tolls one. Expect the second on the next night at the same hour. The third, upon the next night, when the last stroke of twelve has ceased to vibrate. Look to see me no more; and look that, for your own sake, you remember what has passed between us!"

It walked backward from him; and at every step it took, the window raised itself a little, so that, when the apparition reached it, it was wide open.

Scrooge closed the window, and examined the door by which the Ghost had entered. It was double-locked, as he had locked it with his own hands, and the bolts were undisturbed. Scrooge tried to say, "Humbug!" but stopped at the first syllable. And being, from the emotion he had undergone, or the fatigues of the day, or his glimpse of the invisible world, or the dull conversation of the Ghost, or the lateness of the hour, much in need of repose, he went straight to bed, without undressing, and fell asleep on the instant.

Scrooge wakes when the curtains of his bed are drawn aside by a strange figure, childlike but white-haired, who identifies himself as the Ghost of Christmas Past. "Your past," he explains to Scrooge, and he magically transports the old man to another place and time. He sees himself as a young clerk apprenticed to a jolly merchant named Fezziwig. When the business closes on Christmas Eve the apprentices help to clear the warehouse floor for a great party to which Fezziwig has invited both friends and employees. There is music and feasting, but the highlight of the evening is the merry dancing that goes on till nearly midnight.

Scrooge cannot help contrasting this kind man's treatment of his young apprentice with his own gruff words to his clerk a few hours earlier.

The next memory the ghost makes Scrooge relive is a less happy one. A somewhat older Scrooge, hard-working and beginning to taste success, hears a fair but sad-faced girl saying farewell to him.

"Another idol has displaced me," she says, ". . . I have seen your nobler aspirations fall off one by one, until the master passion, Gain, engrosses you. . . I release you. With a full heart, for the love of him you once were."

This is too painful; Scrooge begs the Ghost to leave him and he sinks back into heavy sleep.

The second spirit to visit Scrooge is a genial giant who carries a torch shaped like a horn of plenty, and who identifies himself as the Ghost of Christmas Present.

"Spirit, conduct me where you will," said Scrooge. "I went forth last night on compulsion, and I learnt a lesson which is working now. Tonight, if you have aught to teach me, let me profit by it."

"Touch my robe!"

Scrooge did as he was told, and held it fast.

The room and its contents all vanished instantly, and they stood in the city streets upon a snowy Christmas morning.

Scrooge and the Ghost passed on, invisible, straight to Scrooge's clerk's; and on the threshold of the door the Spirit smiled, and stopped to bless Bob Cratchit's dwelling with the sprinklings of his torch. Think of that! Bob had but fifteen "bob" a week himself; he pocketed on Saturdays but fifteen copies of his Christian name; and yet the Ghost of Christmas Present blessed his four-roomed house!

Then up rose Mrs. Cratchit, Cratchit's wife, dressed out but poorly in a twice-turned gown, but brave in ribbons, which are cheap and make a goodly show for sixpence; and she laid the cloth, assisted by Belinda Cratchit, second of her daughters, also brave in ribbons; while Master Peter Cratchit plunged a fork into the saucepan of potatoes, and, getting the corners of his monstrous shirt collar (Bob's private property, conferred upon his son and heir in honour of the day) into his mouth, rejoiced to find himself so gallantly attired, and yearned to show his linen in the fashionable Parks. And now two smaller Cratchits, boy and girl, came tearing in, screaming that outside the baker's they had smelt the goose, and known it for their own; and, basking in luxurious thoughts of sage and onion, these young Cratchits danced about the table, and exalted Master Peter Cratchit to the skies, while he (not proud, although

The heart is as visible as a dueler's mark, is the best dancer, the most often caught under mistletoe, the bearer of the yule log.

35

his collars nearly choked him) blew the fire, until the slow potatoes, bubbling up, knocked loudly at the saucepan lid to be let out and peeled.

"What has ever got your precious father then?" said Mrs. Cratchit. "And your brother Tiny Tim! And Martha warn't as late last Christmas day by half an hour!"

"Here's Martha, mother!" said a girl, appearing as she spoke.

"Here's Martha, mother!" cried the two young Cratchits. "Hurrah! There's *such* a goose, Martha!"

"Why, bless your heart alive, my dear, how late you are!" said Mrs. Cratchit, kissing her a dozen times, and taking off her shawl and bonnet for her.

"We'd a deal of work to finish up last night," replied the girl, "and had to clear away this morning, mother!"

"Well! Never mind so long as you are come," said Mrs. Cratchit. "Sit ye down before the fire, my dear, and have a warm, Lord bless ye!"

"No, no! There's father coming," cried the two young Cratchits, who were everywhere at once. "Hide, Martha, hide!"

So Martha hid herself, and in came little Bob, the father, with at least three feet of comforter, exclusive of the fringe, hanging down before him; and his threadbare clothes darned up and brushed, to look seasonable; and Tiny Tim upon his shoulder. Alas for Tiny Tim, he bore a little crutch, and had his limbs supported by an iron frame!

"Why, where's our Martha?" cried Bob Cratchit, looking round.

"Not coming," said Mrs. Cratchit.

"Not coming!" said Bob, with a sudden declension in his high spirits; for he had been Tim's blood horse all the way from church, and had come home rampant—"not coming upon Christmas day!"

Martha didn't like to see him disappointed, if it were only in joke; so she came out prematurely from behind the closet door, and ran into his arms, while the two young Cratchits hustled Tiny Tim, and bore him off into the wash house, that he might hear the pudding singing in the copper.

"And how did little Tim behave?" asked Mrs. Cratchit, when she had rallied Bob on his credulity, and Bob had hugged his daughter to his heart's content.

"As good as gold," said Bob, "and better. Somehow he gets thoughtful, sitting by himself so much, and thinks the strangest things you ever heard. He told me, coming home, that he hoped the people saw him in the church, because he was a cripple, and it might be pleasant to them to remember, upon Christmas day, who made lame beggars walk and blind men see."

Bob's voice was tremulous when he told them this, and trembled more when he said that Tiny Tim was growing strong and hearty.

His active little crutch was heard upon the floor, and back came Tiny Tim before another word was spoken, escorted by his brother and sister to his stool beside the fire; and while Bob, turning up his cuffs—as if, poor fellow, they were capable of being made more shabby—compounded some hot mixture in a jug with gin and lemons, and stirred it round and round, and put it on the hob to simmer, Master Peter and the two ubiquitous young Cratchits went to fetch the goose, with which they soon returned in high procession.

Mrs. Cratchit made the gravy (ready beforehand in a little saucepan) hissing hot; Master Peter mashed the potatoes with incredible vigour; Miss Belinda sweetened up the applesauce; Martha dusted the hot plates; Bob took Tiny Tim beside him in a tiny corner at the table; the two young Cratchits set chairs for everybody, not forgetting themselves, and mounting guard upon their posts, crammed spoons into their mouths, lest they should shriek for goose before their turn came to be helped. At last the dishes were set on, and grace was said. It was succeeded by a breathless pause, as Mrs. Cratchit, looking slowly all along the carving knife, prepared to plunge it in the breast; but when she did, and when the long-expected gush of stuffing issued forth, one murmur of delight arose all round the board, and even Tiny Tim, excited by the two young Cratchits, beat on the table with the handle of his knife, and feebly cried, Hurrah!

There never was such a goose. Bob said he didn't believe there ever was such a goose cooked. Its tenderness and flavour, size and cheapness, were the themes of

universal admiration. Eked out by applesauce and mashed potatoes, it was a sufficient dinner for the whole family; indeed, as Mrs. Cratchit said with great delight (surveying one small atom of a bone upon the dish) they hadn't eaten it all at last! Yet everyone had had enough, and the youngest Cratchits in particular were steeped in sage and onion to the eyebrows! But now, the plates being changed by Miss Belinda, Mrs. Cratchit left the room alone—too nervous to bear witnesses—to take the pudding up, and bring it in.

Suppose it should not be done enough! Suppose it should break in turning out! Suppose somebody should have got over the wall of the backyard, and stolen it, while they were merry with the goose—a supposition at which the two young Cratchits became livid! All sorts of horrors were supposed.

Hallo! A great deal of steam! The pudding was out of the copper. A smell like a washing day! That was the cloth. A smell like an eating house and pastry cook's next door to each other, with a laundress's next door to that! That was the pudding! In half a minute Mrs. Cratchit entered—flushed but smiling proudly—with the pudding, like a speckled cannonball, so hard and firm, blazing in half of half a quartern of ignited brandy, and bedight with Christmas holly stuck into the top.

Oh, a wonderful pudding! Bob Cratchit said, and calmly too, that he regarded it as the greatest success achieved by Mrs. Cratchit since their marriage. Mrs. Cratchit said that now the weight was off her mind, she would confess she had had her doubts about the quantity of flour. Everybody had something to say about it, but nobody said or thought it was at all a small pudding for a large family. Any Cratchit would have blushed to hint at such a thing.

At last the dinner was all done, the cloth was cleared, the hearth swept, and the fire made up. The compound in the jug being tasted, and considered perfect, apples and oranges were put upon the table, and a shovelful of chestnuts on the fire.

Then all the Cratchit family drew round the hearth, in what Bob Cratchit called a circle, and at Bob Cratchit's elbow stood the family display of glass—two tumblers, and a small custard cup that was without a handle.

These held the hot stuff from the jug, however, as well as golden goblets would have done; and Bob served it out with beaming looks, while the chestnuts on the fire spluttered and crackled noisily. Then Bob proposed:

"A Merry Christmas to us all, my dears. God bless us!" Which all the family reechoed.

"God bless us every one!" said Tiny Tim, the last of all.

He sat very close to his father's side, upon his little stool. Bob held his withered little hand in his, as if he loved the child, and wished to keep him by his side, and dreaded that he might be taken from him.

Scrooge raised his head speedily, on hearing his own name.

"Mr. Scrooge!" said Bob; "I'll give you Mr. Scrooge, the Founder of the Feast!"

"The Founder of the Feast indeed!" cried Mrs. Cratchit, reddening. "I wish I had him here. I'd give him a piece of my mind to feast upon, and I hope he'd have a good appetite for it."

"My dear," said Bob, "the children! Christmas day."

"It should be Christmas day, I am sure," said she, "on which one drinks the health of such an odious, stingy, hard, unfeeling man as Mr. Scrooge. You know he is, Robert! Nobody knows it better than you do, poor fellow!"

"My dear, " was Bob's mild answer, "Christmas day."

"I'll drink his health for your sake and the day's," said Mrs. Cratchit, "not for his. Long life to him! A merry Christmas and a happy New Year! He'll be very merry and very happy, I have no doubt!"

The children drank the toast after her. It was the first of their proceedings which had no heartiness in it. Tiny Tim drank it last of all, but he didn't care twopence for it. Scrooge was the Ogre of the family. The mention of his name cast a dark shadow on the party, which was not dispelled for full five minutes.

After it had passed away, they were ten times merrier than before, from the mere relief of Scrooge the Baleful being done with. Bob Cratchit told them how he had a situation in his eye for Master Peter, which would bring him, if obtained, full five and sixpence weekly. The two young Cratchits laughed tremendously at the idea of Peter's being a man of business; and Peter himself looked thoughtfully at the fire from between his collars, as if he were deliberating what particular investments he should favour when he came into the receipt of that bewildering income. Martha, who was a poor apprentice at a milliner's, then told them what kind of work she had to do, and how many hours she worked at a stretch, and how she meant to lie abed tomorrow morning for a good long rest; tomorrow being a holiday she passed at home. Also how she had seen a countess and a lord some days before, and how the lord "was much about as tall as Peter"; at which Peter pulled up his collars so high that you couldn't have seen his head if you had been there. All this time the chestnuts and the jug went round and round; and by and by they had a song, about a lost child travelling in the snow, from Tiny Tim, who had a plaintive little voice, and sang it very well indeed.

There was nothing of high mark in this. They were not a handsome family; they were not well dressed; their shoes were far from being waterproof; their clothes were scanty; and Peter might have known, and very likely did, the inside of a pawnbroker's. But they were happy, grateful, pleased with one another, and contented with the time; and when they faded, and looked happier yet in the bright sprinklings of the Spirit's torch at parting, Scrooge had his eye upon them, and especially on Tiny Tim, until the last.

It was a great surprise to Scrooge, as this scene vanished, to hear a hearty laugh. It was a much greater surprise to Scrooge to recognize it as his own nephew's, and to find himself in a bright, dry, gleaming room, with the Spirit standing smiling by his side, and looking at that same nephew.

· It is a fair, evenhanded, noble adjustment of things, that while there is infection in disease and sorrow, there is nothing in the world so irresistibly contagious as laughter and good humour. When Scrooge's nephew laughed, Scrooge's niece by marriage laughed as heartily as he. And their assembled friends, being not a bit behindhand, laughed out lustily.

"He said that Christmas was a humbug, as I live!" cried Scrooge's nephew. "He believed it too!"

"More shame for him, Fred!" said Scrooge's niece, indignantly. Bless those women! they never do anything by halves. They are always in earnest.

She was very pretty; exceedingly pretty. With a dimpled, surprised-looking, capital face; a ripe little mouth that seemed made to be kissed—as no doubt it was; all kinds of good little dots about her chin, that melted into one another when she laughed; and the sunniest pair of eyes you ever saw in any little creature's head. Altogether she was what you would have called provoking, but satisfactory, too. Oh, perfectly satisfactory.

"He's a comical old fellow," said Scrooge's nephew, "that's the truth; and not so pleasant as he might be. However, his offenses carry their own punishment, and I have nothing to say against him. Who suffers by his ill whims? Himself, always. Here he takes it into his head to dislike us, and he won't come and dine with us. What's the consequence? He doesn't lose much of a dinner."

"Indeed, I think he loses a very good dinner," interrupted Scrooge's niece. Everybody else said the same, and they must be allowed to have been competent judges, because they had just had dinner; and, with the dessert upon the table, were clustered round the fire, by lamplight.

"Well, I am very glad to hear it," said Scrooge's nephew, "because I haven't any great faith in these young housekeepers. What do you say, Topper?"

Topper clearly had his eye on one of Scrooge's niece's sisters, for he answered that a bachelor was a wretched outcast, who had no right to express an opinion on the subject. Whereat Scrooge's niece's sister—the plump one with lace tucker; not the one with the roses—blushed.

After tea they had some music. For they were a musical family, and knew what they were about, when they sang a Glee or Catch, I can assure you—especially Topper, who could growl in the bass like a good one.

When this scene vanishes the Ghost of Christmas Yet to Come—a stooped figure shrouded in black—arrives to

"... while there is infection in disease and sorrow, there is nothing in the world so irresistibly contagious as good humor."

conduct Scrooge on yet another tour. This time, Scrooge knows, he will be shown glimpses of his own future. He shudders at the ghost's touch.

"I fear you more than any spectre I have seen," Scrooge says. *"But I know your purpose is to do me good, and as I hope to live to be another man from what I am, I am prepared to bear you company, and do it with a thankful heart."*

Then the spirit transports Scrooge to a city street where he hears men discussing a death, then to a pawn shop where thieves are selling the clothing and bedding of the dead man, and finally to a plundered bedroom where the dead man lies alone, for there is no one to mourn him or sit with the body. The face is concealed but Scrooge guesses that if it were visible he might see his own features.

"Spirit!" he cries. "This is a fearful place. In leaving it, I shall not leave its lesson."

Scrooge is saddened by this grim vision, and he begs the spirit to show him some tenderness connected with death. In response. . . .

The Ghost conducted him to poor Bob Cratchit's house—the dwelling he had visited before—and found the mother and the children seated round the fire.

Quiet. Very quiet. The noisy little Cratchits were as still as statues in one corner, and sat looking up at Peter, who had a book before him. The mother and her daughters were engaged in needlework. But surely they were very quiet!

" 'And he took a child, and set him in the midst of them.' "

Where had Scrooge heard these words? He had not dreamed them. The boy must have read them out, as he and the Spirit crossed the threshold. Why did he not go on?

The mother laid her work upon the table, and put her hand up to her face. "The colour hurts my eyes," she said.

The colour? Ah, poor Tiny Tim!

"They're better now again. It makes them weak by candlelight; and I wouldn't show weak eyes to your father when he comes home. It must be near his time."

"Past it rather," Peter answered, shutting up his book. "But I think he has walked a little slower than he used, these few last evenings, mother."

"I have known him walk with—I have known him walk with Tiny Tim upon his shoulder, very fast indeed."

"And so have I," cried Peter. "Often."

"And so have I," exclaimed another. So had all.

"But he was very light to carry, and his father loved him so, that it was no trouble—no trouble. And there is your father at the door!"

She hurried out to meet him; and little Bob in his comforter—he had need of it, poor fellow—came in. His tea was ready for him on the hob, and they all tried who should help him to it most. Then the two young Cratchits got upon his knees and laid, each child, a little cheek against his face, as if they said, "Don't mind it, father. Don't be grieved!"

Bob was very cheerful with them, and spoke pleasantly to all the family. He looked at the work upon the table, and praised the industry and speed of Mrs. Cratchit and the girls. They would be done long before Sunday, he said.

"Sunday! You went today, then, Robert?"

"Yes, my dear," returned Bob. "I wish you could have gone. It would have done you good to see how green a place it is. But you'll see it often. I promised him that I would walk there on a Sunday. My little, little child! My little child!"

He broke down all at once. He couldn't help it. If he could have helped it, he and his child would have been further apart, perhaps, than they were.

"Spectre," said Scrooge, "something informs me that our parting moment is at hand. I know it, but I know not how. Tell me what man that was, with the covered face, whom we saw lying dead?"

The Ghost of Christmas Yet to Come conveyed him to a dismal, wretched, ruinous churchyard.

The Spirit stood amongst the graves, and pointed down to One.

"Before I draw nearer to that stone to which you

"It was always said of him that he knew how to keep Christmas well, if any man possessed that knowledge. May that be said of us."

point, answer me one question. Are these the shadows of the things that Will be, or are they shadows of the things that May be only?"

Still the Ghost pointed downward to the grave by which it stood.

"Men's courses will foreshadow certain ends, to which, if persevered in, they must lead. But if the courses be departed from, the ends will change. Say it is thus with what you show me!"

The Spirit was immovable as ever.

Scrooge crept towards it, trembling as he went; and, following the finger, read upon the stone of the neglected grave his own name—*Ebenezer Scrooge.*

"Am *I* that man who lay upon the bed? No, Spirit! Oh no, no! Spirit! hear me! I am not the man I was. I will not be the man I must have been but for this intercourse. Why show me this, if I am past all hope? Assure me that I yet may change these shadows you have shown me by an altered life."

For the first time the kind hand faltered.

"I will honour Christmas in my heart, and try to keep it all the year. I will live in the Past, the Present, and the Future. The Spirits of all three shall strive within me. I will not shut out the lessons that they teach. Oh, tell me I may sponge away the writing on this stone!"

Holding up his hands in one last prayer to have his fate reversed, he saw an alteration in the Phantom's hood and dress. It shrank, collapsed, and dwindled down into a bedpost.

Yes, and the bedpost was his own. The bed was his own, the room was his own. Best and happiest of all, the Time before him was his own, to make amends in!

He was checked in his transports by the churches ringing out the lustiest peals he had ever heard.

Running to the window, he opened it, and put out his head. No fog, no mist, no night; clear, bright, stirring, golden day.

"What's today?" cried Scrooge, calling downward to a boy in Sunday clothes, who perhaps had loitered in to look about him.

"*Eh?*"

"What's today, my fine fellow?"

"Today! Why, *Christmas day.*"

"It's Christmas day! I haven't missed it. Hallo, my fine fellow!"

"Hallo!"

"Do you know the Poulterer's, in the next street but one, at the corner?"

"I should hope I did."

"An intelligent boy! A remarkable boy! Do you know whether they've sold the prize Turkey that was hanging up there? Not the little prize turkey—the big one?"

"What, the one as big as me?"

"What a delightful boy! It's a pleasure to talk to him. Yes, my buck!"

"It's hanging there now."

"Is it? Go and buy it."

"Walk-*er!*" exclaimed the boy.

"No, no, I am in earnest. Go and buy it, and tell 'em to bring it here, that I may give them the direction where to take it. Come back with the man, and I'll give you a shilling. Come back with him in less than five minutes, and I'll give you half a crown!"

The boy was off like a shot.

"I'll send it to Bob Cratchit's! He shan't know who sends it. It's twice the size of Tiny Tim. Joe Miller never made such a joke as sending it to Bob's will be!"

The hand in which he wrote the address was not a steady one; but write it he did, somehow, and went downstairs to open the street door, ready for the coming of the poulterer's man.

It *was* a Turkey! He never could have stood upon his legs, that bird. He would have snapped 'em short off in a minute, like sticks of sealing wax.

Scrooge dressed himself "all in his best," and at last got out into the streets. The people were by this time pouring forth, as he had seen them with the Ghost of Christmas Present; and, walking with his hands behind him, Scrooge regarded everyone with a delighted smile. He looked so irresistibly pleasant, in a word, that three or four good-humoured fellows said, "Good morning, sir! A merry Christmas to you!" And Scrooge said often afterwards that, of all the blithe sounds he had ever heard, those were the blithest in his ears.

In the afternoon, he turned his steps toward his nephew's house.

He passed the door a dozen times, before he had the courage to knock. But he made a dash, and did it.

"Is your master at home, my dear?" said Scrooge to the girl. Nice girl! Very.

"Yes, sir."

"Where is he, my love?"

"He's in the dining room, sir, along with mistress."

"He knows me," said Scrooge, with his hand already on the dining-room lock. "I'll go in here, my dear."

"Fred!"

"Why, bless my soul!" cried Fred, "who's that?"

"It's I. Your uncle Scrooge. I have come to dinner. Will you let me in, Fred?"

Let him in! It is a mercy he didn't shake his arm off. He was at home in five minutes. Nothing could be heartier. His niece looked just the same. So did Topper when *he* came. So did the plump sister when *she* came. So did everyone when *they* came. Wonderful party, wonderful games, wonderful unanimity, and happiness!

". . . in his ears, blithe sounds."

But he was early at the office next morning. Oh, he was early there. If he could only be there first, and catch Bob Cratchit coming late! That was the thing he had set his heart upon.

And he did it. The clock struck nine. No Bob. A quarter past. No Bob. Bob was full eighteen minutes and a half behind his time. Scrooge sat with his door wide open, that he might see him come into the tank.

Bob's hat was off before he opened the door; his comforter too. He was on the stool in a jiffy; driving away with his pen, as if he were trying to overtake nine o'clock.

"Hallo!" growled Scrooge, in his accustomed voice, as near as he could possibly feign it. "What do you mean by coming here to my office at this time of the day?"

"I am very sorry, sir. I *am* behind my time."

"You are? Yes. I think you are. Step this way if you please."

"It's only once a year, sir. It shall not be repeated. I was making rather merry yesterday, sir."

"Now, I'll tell you what, my friend. I am not going to stand this sort of thing any longer. And therefore," Scrooge continued, leaping from his stool, and giving Bob such a dig in the waistcoat that he staggered back into the tank again—"and therefore I am about to raise your salary!"

Bob trembled, and got a little nearer to the ruler.

"A merry Christmas, Bob!" said Scrooge, with an earnestness that could not be mistaken, as he clapped him on the back. "A merrier Christmas, Bob, my good fellow, than I have given you for many a year! I'll raise your salary, and endeavour to assist your struggling family, and we will discuss your affairs this very afternoon, over a Christmas bowl of smoking bishop. Make up the fires, and buy a second coal-scuttle before you dot another *i*, Bob!!"

Scrooge was better than his word. He did it all, and infinitely more; and to Tiny Tim, who did *not* die, he was a second father. He became as good a friend, as good a master, and as good a man as the good old city knew, or any other good old city, town, or borough in the good old world. Some people laughed to see the alteration in him; but his heart laughed, and that was enough.

He had no further intercourse with Spirits, but lived in that respect upon the Total Abstinence Principle ever afterwards; and it was always said of him that he knew how to keep Christmas well, if any man alive possessed the knowledge. May that be truly said of us, and all of us! And so, as Tiny Tim observed, God Bless Us, Every One!

Hans Christian Andersen

The Fir Tree

Out in the forest stood a pretty little Fir Tree. It had a good place; it could have sunlight, air there was in plenty, and all around grew many larger comrades—pines as well as firs. But the little Fir Tree wished ardently to become greater. It did not care for the warm sun and the fresh air; it took no notice of the peasant children, who went about talking together, when they had come out to look for strawberries and raspberries. Often they came with a whole potful, or had strung berries on a straw; then they would sit down by the little Fir Tree and say, "How pretty and small that one is!" and the Fir Tree did not like to hear that at all.

Next year he had grown a great joint, and the following year he was longer still, for in fir trees one can always tell by the number of rings they have how many years they have been growing.

"Oh, if I were only as great a tree as the other!" sighed the little Fir, "then I would spread my branches far around, and look out from my crown into the wide world. The birds would then build nests in my boughs, and when the wind blew I could nod just as grandly as the others yonder."

It took no pleasure in the sunshine, in the birds, and in the red clouds that went sailing over him morning and evening.

When it was winter, and the snow lay all around, white and sparkling, a hare would often come jumping along, and spring right over the little Fir Tree. Oh! this made him so angry. But two winters went by, and when the third came the little Tree had grown so tall that the hare was obliged to run around it.

"Oh! to grow, to grow, and become old; that's the only fine thing in the world," thought the Tree.

In the autumn woodcutters always came and felled a few of the largest trees; that was done this year too, and the little Fir Tree, that was now quite well grown, shuddered with fear, for the great stately trees fell to the ground with a crash, and their branches were cut off, so that the trees looked quite naked, long, and slender—they could hardly be recognized. But then they were laid upon wagons, and horses dragged them away out of the wood. Where were they going? What destiny awaited them in the unknown world that lies beyond the forest?

In the spring, when the Swallows and the Stork came, the Tree asked them, "Do you know where they were taken? Did you not meet them?"

The Swallows knew nothing about it, but the Stork looked thoughtful, nodded his head, and said:

"Yes, I think so. I met many new ships when I flew out of Egypt; on this ships were stately masts; I fancy these were the trees. They smelled like fir. I can assure you they're stately—very stately."

"Oh that I were only big enough to go over the sea! What kind of thing is this sea, and how does it look?"

"It would take too long to explain all that," said the Stork, and he went away.

"Rejoice in thy youth," said the Sunbeams; "rejoice in thy fresh growth, and in the young life that is within thee."

And the wind kissed the Tree, and the dew wept tears upon it; but the Fir Tree did not understand that.

When Christmastime approached, quite young trees were felled, sometimes trees which were neither so old nor so large as this Fir Tree, that never rested, but always wanted to go away. These young trees, which were always the most beautiful, kept all their branches; they were put upon wagons, and horses dragged them away out of the wood.

"Where are they all going?" asked the Fir Tree. "They are not greater than I—indeed, one of them was much smaller. Why do they keep all their branches? Whither are they taken?"

"We know that! We know that!" chirped the Sparrows. "Yonder in the town we looked in at the windows. We know where they go. Oh! they are dressed up in the greatest pomp and splendor that can be imagined. We have looked in at the windows, and have perceived that they are planted in the middle of a warm room, and adorned with the most beautiful things—gilt apples, honey cakes, playthings, and many hundred candles."

"And then?" asked the Fir Tree, and trembled through all its branches. "And then? What happens then?"

"Why, we have not seen anything more. But it was

Christmas is the time of the nose.
The clean frost of the forest, the sharp green
of cedar and fir scent the joyous season.

Norman
Rockwell

From the forests, from roadside stands, on car tops, on backs, in little red wagons, the tree reaches out with branches of happiness.

incomparable, all the warm brightness and the beauty."

"Perhaps I may be destined to tread this glorious path one day!" cried the Fir Tree, rejoicingly. "That is even better than traveling across the sea. How painfully I long for it! If it were only Christmas now! Now I am great and grown up, like the rest who were led away last year. Oh, if I were only on the carriage! If I were only in the warm room, among all the pomp and splendor! And then? Yes, then something even better will come, something far more charming, or else why should they adorn me so? There must be something grander, something greater still to come; but what? Oh! I'm suffering, I'm longing! I don't know myself what is the matter with me!"

"Rejoice in us," said Air and Sunshine. "Rejoice in thy fresh youth here in the woodland."

But the Fir Tree did not rejoice at all, but it grew and grew; winter and summer it stood there, green, dark green. The people who saw it said, "That's a handsome

tree!" and at Christmastime it was felled before any one of the others. The ax cut deep into its marrow, and the tree fell to the ground with a sigh; it felt a pain, a sensation of faintness, and could not think at all of happiness, for it was sad at parting from its home, from the place where it had grown up; it knew that it should never again see the dear old companions, the little bushes and flowers all around—perhaps not even the birds. The parting was not at all agreeable.

The Tree only came to itself when it was unloaded in a yard, with other trees, and heard a man say:

"This one is famous; we want only this one!"

Now two servants came in gay liveries, and carried the Fir Tree into a large, beautiful saloon. All around the walls were hung pictures, and by the great stove stood large Chinese vases with lions on the covers; there were rocking chairs, silken sofas, great tables covered with picture books, and toys worth a hundred times a hun-

Christmas trees are a beautiful importation from Germany.
The custom of having them is now widespread, even in Puritan New England.
What a forest of brilliantly bedecked evergreen would be visible
were all the firs that are to be laden and lighted this year brought together;
and what a story that forest would tell of busy hands, and buzzing consultations;
of secrets it was hard to keep; of restless expectations and wistful looks;
of the joy of givers and the gladness of receivers;
of, in a word, the merry sympathy of warm affection.

THE SATURDAY EVENING POST, DECEMBER 28, 1867

Against the dark boughs the candles glow with the hopes and promises of the new year. Even the most cynical men still resolve to change.

dred dollars, at least the children said so. And the Fir Tree was put into a great tub filled with sand; but no one could see that it was a tub, for it was hung round with green cloth, and stood on a large, many-colored carpet. Oh, how the Tree trembled! What was to happen now? The servants, and the young ladies also, decked it out. On one branch they hung little nets, cut out of colored paper; every net was filled with sweetmeats; golden apples and walnuts hung down, as if they grew there, and more than a hundred little candles, red, white, and blue, were fastened to the different boughs. Dolls that looked exactly like real people—the tree had never seen such before—swung among the foliage, and high on the summit of the Tree was fixed a tinsel star. It was splendid, particularly splendid.

"This evening," said all, "this evening it will shine."

"Oh," thought the Tree, "that it were evening already! Oh, that the lights may be soon lit up! When may that be done? I wonder if trees will come out of the forest to look at me? Will the sparrows fly against the panes? Shall I grow fast here, and stand adorned in summer and winter?"

Yes, he did not guess badly. But he had a complete backache from mere longing, and the backache is just as bad for a Tree as the headache for a person.

At last the candles were lighted. What a brilliance, what splendor! The Tree trembled so in all its branches that one of the candles set fire to a green twig, and it was scorched.

"Heaven preserve us!" cried the young ladies; and they hastily put the fire out.

Now the Tree might not even tremble. Oh, that was terrible! It was so afraid of setting fire to some of its ornaments and it was quite bewildered with all the brilliance. And now the folding doors were thrown open, and a number of children rushed in as if they would have overturned the whole Tree; the older people followed more deliberately. The little ones stood quite silent, but only for a minute; then they shouted till the room rang: they danced gleefully round the Tree, and one present after another was plucked from it.

"What are they about?" thought the Tree. "What's going to be done? What wonderful things happen next?"

And the candles burned down to the twigs, and as they burned down they were extinguished, and then the children received permission to plunder the Tree. Oh! they rushed in upon it, so that every branch cracked again: if it had not been fastened by the top and by the golden star to the ceiling, it would have fallen down.

The children danced about with their pretty toys. No one looked at the Tree except one old man, who came up and peeped among the branches, but only to see if a fig or an apple had not been forgotten.

"A story! A story!" shouted the children; and they drew a little fat man toward the tree; and he sat down just beneath it—"for then we shall be in the green wood," said he, "and the tree may have the advantage of listening to my tale. But I can only tell one. Will you hear the story of Ivede-Avede, or of Klumpey-Dumpey, who fell downstairs, and still was raised up to honor and married the Princess?"

"Ivede-Avede!" cried some, "Klumpey-Dumpey!" cried others, and there was a great crying and shouting. Only the Fir Tree was quite silent, and thought, "Shall I not be in it? Shall I have nothing to do in it?" But he had been in the evening's amusement, and had done what was required of him.

And the fat man told about Klumpey-Dumpey who fell downstairs, and yet was raised to honor and married the Princess. And the children clapped their hands, and cried, "Tell another! tell another!" for they wanted to hear about Ivede-Avede; but they only got the story of Klumpey-Dumpey. The Fir Tree stood quite silent and thoughtful; never had the birds in the wood told such a story as that. Klumpey-Dumpey fell downstairs, and yet came to honor and married the Princess!

"Yes, so it happens in the world!" thought the Fir Tree, and believed it must be true, because that was such a nice man who told it. "Well, who can know? Perhaps I shall fall downstairs, too, and marry a Princess!" And it looked forward with pleasure to being adorned again, the next evening, with candles and toys, gold and fruit. "Tomorrow I shall not tremble," it thought.

"I will rejoice in all my splendor. Tomorrow I shall

The joy of children finding the perfect
tree in their own woods and bringing it home
is portrayed by Post artist John Clymer.

One thing is certain, fate would never bestow a fire upon this engine company at this particular moment.

hear the story of Klumpey-Dumpey again, and perhaps that of Ivede-Avede, too."

And the Tree stood all night quiet and thoughtful.

In the morning the servants and the chambermaid came in.

"Now my splendor will begin afresh," thought the Tree. But they dragged him out of the room, and upstairs to the garret, and here they put him in a dark corner where no daylight shone.

"What's the meaning of this?" thought the Tree. "What am I to do here? What is to happen?"

And he leaned against the wall, and thought, and

thought. And he had time enough, for days and nights went by and nobody came up; and when at length someone came, it was only to put some great boxes in a corner. Now the Tree stood quite hidden away, and the supposition is that it was quite forgotten.

"Now it's winter outside," thought the Tree. "The earth is hard and covered with snow, and people cannot plant me; therefore I suppose I'm to be sheltered here until spring comes. How considerate that is! How good people are! If it were only not so dark here, and so terribly solitary!—not even a little hare? That was pretty out there in the wood, when the snow lay thick and the

Christmas is a group effort in small towns across the country, a pouring forth of community spirit.

hare sprang past; yes, even when he jumped over me; but then I did not like it. It is terribly lonely up here!"

"Peep! peep!" said a little Mouse, and crept forward, and then came another little one. They smelled at the Fir Tree, and then slipped among the branches.

"It's horribly cold," said the two little Mice, "or else it would be comfortable here. Don't you think so, you old Fir Tree?"

"I'm not old at all," said the Fir Tree. "There are many much older than I."

"Where do you come from?" asked the Mice. "And what do you know?" They were dreadfully inquisitive.

"Tell us about the most beautiful spot on earth. Have you been there? Have you been in the storeroom, where cheeses lie on the shelves, and hams hang from the ceiling, where one dances on tallow candles, and goes in thin and comes out fat?"

"I don't know that," replied the Tree; "but I know the wood, where the sun shines and the birds sing."

And then it told all about its youth.

And the little Mice had never heard anything of the kind; and they listened and said:

"What a number of things you have seen! How happy you must have been!"

51

"I?" replied the Fir Tree; and it thought about what it had told. "Yes, those were really quite happy times." But then he told of the Christmas Eve when he had been hung with sweetmeats and candles.

"Oh!" said the little Mice, "how happy you have been, you old Fir Tree!"

"I'm not old at all," said the Tree. "I only came out of the wood this winter. I'm only rather backward in my growth."

"What splendid stories you can tell!" said the little Mice.

And next night they came with four other little Mice, to hear what the Tree had to relate; and the more it said, the more clearly did it remember everything, and thought, "Those were quite merry days! But they may come again. Klumpey-Dumpey fell downstairs, and yet he married the Princess. Perhaps I may marry a Princess too!" And the Fir Tree thought of a pretty little Birch Tree that grew out in the forest; and for the Fir Tree, that Birch was a real Princess.

"Who's Klumpey-Dumpey?" asked the little Mice.

And then the Fir Tree told the whole story. It could remember every single word; and the little Mice were ready to leap to the very top of the tree with pleasure. Next night a great many more Mice came, and on Sunday two Rats even appeared; but these thought the story was not pretty, and the little Mice were sorry for that, for now they also did not like it so much as before.

"Do you know only one story?" asked the Rats.

"Only that one," replied the Tree. "I heard that on the happiest evening of my life; I did not think then how happy I was."

"That's a very miserable story. Don't you know any about bacon and tallow candles—a storeroom story?"

"No," said the Tree.

"Then we'd rather not hear you," said the Rats.

And they went back to their own people. The little Mice at last stayed away also; and then the Tree sighed and said:

"It was very nice when they sat round me, the merry little Mice, and listened when I spoke to them. Now that's past too. But I shall remember to be pleased when they come to take me out of this dark, tiresome place."

But when did that happen? Why, it was one morning that people came and rummaged in the garret: the boxes were put away, and the Tree brought out; they certainly threw him rather roughly on the floor, but a servant dragged him away at once to the stairs, where the daylight shone.

"Now life is beginning again!" thought the Tree.

It felt the fresh air and the first sunbeams, and now it was out in the courtyard. Everything passed so quickly that the Tree quite forgot to look at itself, there was so much to look at all round. The courtyard was close to a garden, and here everything was blooming; the roses hung fresh and fragrant over the little paling, the linden trees were in blossom, and the swallows cried, "Quinze-wit! quinze-wit! my husband's come!" But it was not the Fir Tree that they meant.

"Now I shall live!" said the Tree, rejoicingly, and spread its branches far out; but, alas! they were all withered and yellow; and it lay in the corner among nettles and weeds. The tinsel star was still upon it, and shone in the bright sunshine.

In the courtyard a couple of the merry children were playing who had danced round the tree at Christmas-time, and had rejoiced over it. One of the youngest ran up and tore off the golden star.

"Look what is sticking to the ugly old fir tree!" said the child, and he trod upon the branches till they cracked again under his boots.

And the Tree looked at all the blooming flowers and the splendor of the garden, and then looked at itself, and wished it had remained in the dark corner of the garret; it thought of its fresh youth in the wood, of the merry Christmas Eve, and of the little Mice which had listened so pleasantly to the story of Klumpey-Dumpey.

"Past! past!" said the old Tree. "Had I but rejoiced when I could have done so! Past! Past!"

And the servant came and chopped the Tree into little pieces; a whole bundle lay there; it blazed brightly under the great brewing copper, and it sighed deeply, and each sigh was like a little shot; and the children who were at play there ran up and seated themselves at the fire, looked into it, and cried, "Puff! puff!" But at each explosion, which was a deep sigh, the Tree thought of a summer day in the woods, or of a winter night there, when the stars beamed; he thought of Christmas Eve and of Klumpey Dumpey, the only story he had ever heard or knew how to tell; and then the Tree was burned.

The boys played in the garden, and the youngest had on his breast a golden star, which the Tree had worn on its happiest evening. Now that was past, and the Tree's life was past, and the story is past too: past! past!—and that's the way with all stories.

The memory of Christmas is as sweet as the thirst for it; the respite from school, master and books, is manna to live on.

53

O. Henry

The Gift of the Magi

One dollar and eighty-seven cents. That was all. And sixty cents was in pennies. Pennies saved one and two at a time by bulldozing the grocer and the vegetable man and the butcher until one's cheeks burned with the silent imputation of parsimony that such close dealing implied. Three times Della counted it. One dollar and eighty-seven cents. And the next day would be Christmas.

There was clearly nothing to do but flop down on the shabby little couch and howl. So Della did it. Which instigates the moral reflection that life is made up of sobs, sniffles and smiles, with sniffles predominating.

While the mistress of the home is gradually subsiding from the first stage to the second, take a look at the home. A furnished flat at $8.00 per week. It did not exactly beggar description, but it certainly had that word on the lookout for the mendicancy squad.

In the vestibule below was a letter box into which no letter would go, and an electric button from which no mortal finger could coax a ring. Also appertaining thereunto was a card bearing the name "Mr. James Dillingham Young."

The "Dillingham" had been flung to the breeze during a former period of prosperity when its possessor was being paid $30 per week. Now, when the income was shrunk to $20, the letters of "Dillingham" looked blurred, as though they were thinking seriously of contracting to a modest and unassuming D. But whenever Mr. James Dillingham Young came home and reached his flat above he was called "Jim" and greatly hugged by Mrs. James Dillingham Young, already introduced to you as Della. Which is all very good.

Della finished her cry and attended to her cheeks with the powder rag. She stood by the window and looked out dully at a gray cat walking a gray fence in a gray backyard. Tomorrow would be Christmas Day, and she had only $1.87 with which to buy Jim a present. She had been saving every penny she could for months, with this result. Twenty dollars a week doesn't go far. Expenses had been greater than she had calculated. They always are. Only $1.87 to buy a present for Jim. Her Jim. Many a happy hour she had spent planning for something nice for him. Something fine and rare and sterling—something just a little bit near to being worthy of the honor of being owned by James Dillingham Young.

The holiday mood was a sentimental one, in the early 1900's.

There was a pier-glass between the windows of the room. Perhaps you have seen a pier-glass in an $8.00 flat. A very thin and very agile person may, by observing his reflection in a rapid sequence of longitudinal strips, obtain a fairly accurate conception of his looks. Della, being slender, had mastered the art.

Suddenly she whirled from the window and stood before the glass. Her eyes were shining brilliantly, but her face had lost its color within twenty seconds. Rapidly she pulled down her hair and let it fall to its full length.

Now, there were two possessions of the James Dillingham Youngs in which they both took a mighty pride. One was Jim's gold watch that had been his father's and his grandfather's. The other was Della's hair. Had the Queen of Sheba lived in the flat across the airshaft, Della would have let her hair hang out the window some day to dry just to depreciate Her Majesty's jewels and gifts. Had King Solomon been the janitor, with all his treasures piled up in the basement, Jim would have pulled out his watch every time he passed, just to see him pluck at his beard from envy.

So now Della's beautiful hair fell about her, rippling and shining like a cascade of brown waters. It reached

The beautiful tresses, thick and shining, were the crown of Della's happiness, a happiness based on the happiness they gave her Jim.

below her knee and made itself almost a garment for her. And then she did it up again nervously and quickly. Once she faltered for a minute and stood still while a tear or two splashed on the worn red carpet.

On went her old brown jacket; on went her old brown hat.

With a whirl of skirts and with the brilliant sparkle still in her eyes, she fluttered out the door and down the stairs to the street.

Where she stopped the sign read: "Mme. Sofronie. Hair Goods of All Kinds."

One flight up Della ran, and collected herself, panting. Madame, large, too white, chilly, hardly looked the "Sofronie."

"Will you buy my hair?" asked Della.

"I buy hair," said Madame. "Take yer hat off and let's have a sight at the looks of it."

Down rippled the brown cascade.

"Twenty dollars," said Madame, lifting the mass with a practiced hand.

"Give it to me quick," said Della.

Oh, and the next two hours tripped by on rosy wings. Forget the hashed metaphor. She was ransacking the stores for Jim's present.

She found it at last. It surely had been made for Jim and no one else. There was no other like it in any of the stores, and she had turned all of them inside out. It was a platinum fob chain simple and chaste in design, properly proclaiming its value by substance alone and not by meretricious ornamentation—as all good things should do. It was even worthy of The Watch. As soon as she saw it she knew that it must be Jim's. It was like him. Quietness and value—the description applied to both. Twenty-one dollars they took from her for it, and she hurried home with the eighty-seven cents. With that chain on his watch Jim might be properly anxious about the time in any company.

Grand as the watch was, he sometimes looked at it on the sly on account of the old leather strap that he used in place of a chain.

When Della reached home her intoxication gave way a little to prudence and reason. She got out her curling irons and lighted the gas and went to work repairing the ravages made by generosity added to love. Which is always a tremendous task, dear friends—a mammoth task.

Within forty minutes her head was covered with tiny, close-lying curls that made her look wonderfully like a truant schoolboy. She looked at her reflection in the mirror long, carefully, and critically.

"If Jim doesn't kill me," she said to herself, "before he takes a second look at me, he'll say I look like a Coney Island chorus girl. But what could I do—oh! what could I do with a dollar and eighty-seven cents?"

At seven o'clock the coffee was made and the frying pan was on the back of the stove hot and ready to cook the chops.

Jim was never late. Della doubled the fob chain in her hand and sat on the corner of the table near the door that he always entered. Then she heard his step on the stair away down on the first flight, and she turned white for just a moment. She had a habit of saying little silent prayers about the simplest everyday things, and now she whispered, "Please God, make him think I am still pretty."

The door opened and Jim stepped in and closed it. He looked thin and very serious. Poor fellow, he was only twenty-two—and to be burdened with a family! He needed a new overcoat and he was without gloves.

Jim stopped inside the door, as immovable as a setter at the scent of quail. His eyes were fixed upon Della, and there was an expression in them that she could not read, and it terrified her. It was not anger, nor surprise, nor disapproval, nor horror, nor any of the sentiments that she had been prepared for.

He simply stared at her fixedly with that peculiar expression on his face.

Della wriggled off the table and went for him.

"Jim, darling," she cried, "don't look at me that way. I had my hair cut off and sold it because I couldn't have lived through Christmas without giving you a present. It'll grow out again—you won't mind, will you? I just had to do it. My hair grows awfully fast. Say 'Merry Christmas!' Jim, and let's be happy. You don't know what a nice, what a beautiful, wonderful gift I've got for you."

"You've cut off your hair?" asked Jim, laboriously, as if he had not arrived at that patent fact yet even after the hardest mental labor.

"Cut if off and sold it," said Della. "Don't you like me just as well, anyhow? I'm me without my hair, ain't I?"

Jim looked about the room curiously.

"You say your hair is gone?" he said, with an air almost of idiocy.

"You needn't look for it," said Della. "It's sold, I tell you—sold and gone, too. It's Christmas Eve, boy. Be good to me, for it went for you. Maybe the hairs of my head were numbered," she went on with a sudden serious sweetness, "but nobody could ever count my love for you. Shall I put the chops on, Jim?"

Out of his trance Jim seemed quickly to wake. He enfolded his Della. For ten seconds let us regard with discreet scrutiny some inconsequential object in the other direction.

Eight dollars a week or a million a year—what is the difference?

A mathematician or a wit would give you the wrong answer. The Magi brought valuable gifts, but that was not among them. This dark assertion will be illuminated later on.

Jim drew a package from his overcoat pocket and threw it upon the table.

"Don't make any mistake, Dell," he said, "about me. I don't think there's anything in the way of a haircut or a shave or a shampoo that could make me like my girl any less.

"But if you'll unwrap that package you may see why you had me going a while at first."

White fingers and nimble tore at the string and paper. And then an ecstatic scream of joy; and then, alas! a quick feminine change to hysterical tears and wails, necessitating the immediate employment of all the comforting powers of the lord of the flat.

For there lay The Combs—the set of combs, side and back, that Della had worshipped for long in a Broadway window.

Beautiful combs, pure tortoise shell, with jeweled rims—just the shade to wear in the beautiful vanished hair.

They were expensive combs, she knew, and her heart had simply craved and yearned over them without the least hope of possession. And now, they were hers, but the tresses that should have adorned the coveted adornments were gone.

But she hugged them to her bosom, and at length she was able to look up with dim eyes and a smile and say: "My hair grows so fast, Jim!"

And then Della leaped up like a little singed cat and cried, "Oh, oh!"

Jim had not yet seen his beautiful present. She held it out to him eagerly upon her open palm. The dull precious metal seemed to flash with a reflection of her bright and ardent spirit.

"Isn't it a dandy, Jim? I hunted all over town to find it. You'll have to look at the time a hundred times a day now. Give me your watch. I want to see how it looks on it."

Instead of obeying, Jim tumbled down on the couch and put his hands under the back of his head and smiled in an odd way.

"Dell," said he, "let's put our Christmas presents away and keep 'em a while. They're too nice to use just at present.

"I sold the watch to get the money to buy your combs. And now suppose you put the chops on."

The Magi, as you know, were wise men—wonderfully wise men—who brought gifts to the Babe in the manger. They invented the art of giving Christmas presents. Being wise, their gifts were no doubt wise ones, possibly bearing the privilege of exchange in case of duplication. And here I have lamely related to you the uneventful chronicle of two foolish children in a flat who most unwisely sacrificed for each other the greatest treasures of their house.

But in a last word to the wise of these days let it be said that of all who give gifts these two were the wisest.

Everywhere they are wisest.

They are the magi.

George Horace Lorimer

The Child Who Is King

On a time when Rupert the Good King reigned over the City in the Forests, he decreed that, throughout all his realm, there should be no sorrow nor lack of cheer on Christmas Day.

For be it known that at the Christmastime the Christ Child comes down to earth, and passes from house to house, bringing joy and peace to the poor and lowly. And always on that day sat the king among his knights, waiting in state for the coming of the Child, that he might do Him honor and reverence. And always it befell that night found him sad and silent because the Child had passed him by. For ever are the poor the first care of the Christ, and in the City in the Forests they were many.

Now it being again the eve of Christmas, the king sent his servants through the city, giving to all of his bounty, that none might be without the comfort and the cheer of the holy time. For he reasoned that, if there were no sorrow to stay the Child as He passed through the city, He would come at last to the castle. And Rupert made ready the court to receive Him, and never was braver sight seen in all Christendom.

Now there was in the king's household a jester of most excellent wit, who made much seemly diversion for his master. And he, being in the streets on Christmas Eve, playing divers merry tricks on the simple people, had chanced upon a boy making a loud outcry. For he had wandered off from the monastery where the good fathers cared for the homeless, and knew not the way thither again. Him quieted the jester with fair words, and brought him secretly to the castle, and locked him in a chamber in the tower, where none went, and there left him sleeping. For he thought to clothe him in the motley on the morrow, and thereby make a merry jest for all the little children of the court.

Full soon the midnight bells, that through the year tolled out the passing days, rang joyously, and all the East was radiant with the Star. Upon the hills the sheep in slow procession walked, and in their stalls the oxen fell upon their knees, and Heaven and Earth sang one harmonious song, praising the Child.

Right proudly in his hall sat Rupert, upon his head a crown of gold, and o'er his mail the royal robe of purple. And at his back were threescore valiant knights in shining armor clad. Through all the night they sat there, stiff and silent, and when the dawn stole down it found them waiting.

Then sang the white-robed choir a greeting to the day, and mounting up, the music woke the boy, that through the night had slept unharmed. Long lay he still and listened, and once he called aloud, but there was none to answer back. For the jester was but a light fellow, and overnight he had forgotten.

And now the boy grew frightened, and, standing up, looked out into the court. Across the way he gazed into a room where all the children of the castle stood round a noble fir, full fair with glittering toys and shining lights. To them called he: "Oh, children, come for me, that I may play around the tree"; but there was none to hear, so loud they sang their praises.

Down to the ledge a sparrow flew, and looked in wondering at the boy. "Oh, sparrow, stay with me," he cried in his sorrow and fear, "for I am all alone"; but quick the bird flew off, for everywhere were crumbs thrown out for him and waiting.

Then to the snowflakes, scurrying by, the boy called out: "Fly not so fast away, oh, snowflakes; stay here a while with me." But whirled they on the faster, for in every window there were sights to see.

And now the boy was grieved, that he alone in all the city was forgotten. But of a sudden, above the chanting of the choir, he heard a voice that called his name, and wondering, turned and saw that all the grayness of the granite walls was yellowed into gold, and in a corner stood a tree that glittered with a thousand lights. But, best of all, he saw a little child, who smiled and beckoned him with rosy fingers. And all that day they played together.

Slow dragged the day along, but to the waiting king the Child came not. But as the evening fell, he saw the Star mount up the eastern skies and hang above the tower.

"The Child is coming!" cried the King. "The Child is coming!" echoed all his knights, and every eye glanced

Compelled to mount guard, the lonely soldier knows the great stories of Christmas only through the pantomime of the revelers within.

have no need to visit mine; so I am quite as neglected as you are."

"And all because of this person they call Santa Claus!" exclaimed the Daemon of Envy. "He is simply ruining our business, and something must be done at once."

To this they readily agreed; but what to do was another and more difficult matter to settle. They knew that Santa Claus worked all through the year at his castle in the Laughing Valley, preparing the gifts he was to distribute on Christmas Eve; and at first they resolved to try to tempt him into their caves, that they might lead him on to the terrible pitfalls that ended in destruction.

So the very next day, while Santa Claus was busily at work, surrounded by his little band of assistants, the Daemon of Selfishness came to him and said, "These toys are wonderfully bright and pretty. Why do you not keep them for yourself? It's a pity to give them to those noisy boys and fretful girls, who break and destroy them so quickly."

"Nonsense!" cried the old graybeard, his bright eyes twinkling merrily as he turned toward the tempting Daemon; "the boys and girls are never so noisy and fretful after receiving my presents, and if I can make them happy for one day in the year I am quite content."

So the Daemon went back to the others, who awaited him in their caves, and said, "I have failed, for Santa Claus is not at all selfish."

The following day the Daemon of Envy visited Santa Claus. Said he, "The toy shops are full of playthings quite as pretty as these you are making. What a shame it is that they should interfere with your business! They make toys by machinery much quicker than you can make them by hand; and they sell them for money, while you get nothing at all for your work."

But Santa Claus refused to be envious of the toy shops.

"I can supply the little ones but once a year—on Christmas Eve," he answered; "for the children are many, and I am but one. And as my work is one of love and kindness I would be ashamed to receive money for my little gifts. But throughout all the year the children

must be amused in some way, and so the toy shops are able to bring much happiness to my little friends. I like the toy shops, and am glad to see them prosper."

In spite of this second rebuff, the Daemon of Hatred thought he would try to influence Santa Claus. So the next day he entered the busy workshop and said, "Good morning, Santa! I have bad news for you."

"Then run away, like a good fellow," answered Santa Claus. "Bad news is something that should be kept secret and never told."

"You cannot escape this, however," declared the Daemon; "for in the world are a good many who do not believe in Santa Claus, and these you are bound to hate bitterly, since they have so wronged you."

"Stuff and rubbish!" cried Santa.

"And there are others who resent your making children happy and who sneer at you and call you a foolish old rattlepate! You are quite right to hate such base slanderers, and you ought to be revenged upon them for their evil words."

"But I *don't* hate 'em!" exclaimed Santa Claus, positively. "Such people do me no real harm, but merely render themselves and their children unhappy. Poor things! I'd much rather help them than injure them."

Indeed, the Daemons could not tempt old Santa Claus in any way. On the contrary, he was shrewd enough to see that their object in visiting him was to make mischief and trouble. So the Daemons abandoned honeyed words and determined to use force.

It is well known that no harm can come to Santa Claus while he is in the Laughing Valley, for the fairies, and ryls, and knooks all protect him. But on Christmas Eve he drives his reindeer out into the big world, carrying a sleigh-load of toys and pretty gifts to the children; and this was the time and the occasion when his enemies had the best chance to injure him. So the Daemons laid their plans and awaited the arrival of Christmas Eve.

The moon shone big and white in the sky, and the snow lay crisp and sparkling on the ground as Santa Claus cracked his whip and sped away out of the Valley into the great world beyond. The roomy sleigh was packed full with huge sacks of toys, and as the reindeer

The world is his province; he knows his territory better than astrologers or meteorologists, knows each child by name and age.

dashed onward our jolly old Santa laughed and whistled and sang for very joy. For in all his merry life this was the one day in the year when he was happiest—the day he lovingly bestowed the treasures of his workshop upon the little children.

It would be a busy night for him, he well knew. As he whistled and shouted and cracked his whip again, he reviewed in mind all the towns and cities and farmhouses where he was expected, and figured that he had just enough presents to go around and make every child happy. The reindeer knew exactly what was expected of them, and dashed along so swiftly that their feet scarcely seemed to touch the snow-covered ground.

Suddenly a strange thing happened: a rope shot through the moonlight and a big noose that was in the end of it settled over the arms and body of Santa Claus and drew tight. Before he could resist or even cry out he was jerked from the seat of the sleigh and tumbled head foremost into a snowbank, while the reindeer rushed onward with the load of toys and carried it quickly out of sight and sound.

Such a surprising experience confused old Santa for a moment, and when he had collected his senses he found that the wicked Daemons had pulled him from the snowdrift and bound him tightly with many coils of the stout rope. And then they carried the kidnapped Santa Claus away to their mountain, where they thrust the prisoner into a secret cave and chained him to the rocky wall so that he could not escape.

"Ha, ha!" laughed the Daemons, rubbing their hands together with cruel glee. "What will the children do now? How they will cry and scold and storm when they find there are no toys in their stockings and no gifts on their Christmas trees! And what a lot of punishment they will receive from their parents, and how they will flock to our caves of Selfishness, and Envy, and Hatred, and Malice! We have done a mighty clever thing, we Daemons of the Caves!"

Now it so chanced that on this Christmas Eve the good Santa Claus had taken with him in his sleigh Nuter the Ryl, Peter the Knook, Kilter the Pixie, and a small fairy named Wisk—his four favorite assistants. These little

people he had often found very useful in helping him to distribute his gifts to the children, and when their master was so suddenly dragged from the sleigh they were all snugly tucked underneath the seat, where the sharp wind could not reach them.

The tiny immortals knew nothing of the capture of Santa Claus until some time after he had disappeared. But finally they missed his cheery voice, and as their master always sang or whistled on his journeys, the silence warned them that something was wrong.

Little Wisk stuck out his head from underneath the seat and found Santa Claus gone and no one to direct the flight of the reindeer.

"Whoa!" he called out, and the deer obediently slackened speed and came to a halt.

Peter and Nuter and Kilter all jumped upon the seat and looked back over the track made by the sleigh. But Santa Claus had been left miles and miles behind.

"What shall we do?" asked Wisk, anxiously, all the mirth and mischief banished from his wee face by this great calamity.

"We must go back at once and find our master," said Nuter the Ryl, who thought and spoke with much deliberation.

"No, no!" exclaimed Peter the Knook, who, cross and crabbed though he was, might always be depended upon in an emergency. "If we delay, or go back, there will not be time to get the toys to the children before morning; and that would grieve Santa Claus more than anything else."

"It is certain that some wicked creatures have captured him," added Kilter, thoughtfully; "and their object must be to make the children unhappy. So our first duty is to get the toys distributed as carefully as if Santa Claus were himself present. Afterward we can search for our master and easily secure his freedom."

This seemed such good and sensible advice that the others at once resolved to adopt it. So Peter the Knook called to the reindeer, and the faithful animals again sprang forward and dashed over hill and valley, through forest and plain, until they came to the houses wherein children lay sleeping and dreaming of pretty gifts they

DRAWN BY
SARAH S. STILWELL WEBER

Play is a basic instinct, like survival, continuity. The child is father of the man; the mature mind thrives on its own invention.

would find in their stockings on Christmas morning.

The little immortals had set themselves a difficult task; for although they had assisted Santa Claus on many of his journeys, their master had always directed and guided them and told them exactly what he wished them to do. But now they had to distribute the toys according to their own judgment, and they did not understand children as well as did old Santa. So it is no wonder they made some laughable errors.

Mamie Brown, who wanted a doll, got a drum instead; and a drum is of no use to a girl who loves dolls. And Charlie Smith, who delights to romp and play out of doors, and who wanted some new rubber boots to keep his feet dry, received a sewing box filled with colored worsteds and threads and needles, which made him so provoked that he thoughtlessly called our dear Santa Claus a fraud.

Had there been many such mistakes the Daemons would have accomplished their evil purpose and made the children unhappy. But the little friends of the absent Santa Claus labored faithfully and intelligently to carry out their master's ideas, and they made fewer errors than might be expected under such unusual circumstances.

And, although they worked as swiftly as possible, day had begun to break before the toys and other presents were all distributed; so for the first time in many years the reindeer trotted into the Laughing Valley, on their return, in broad daylight, with the brilliant sun peeping over the edge of the forest to prove they were far behind their accustomed hour.

Having put the deer in the stable, the little folk began to wonder how they might rescue their master; and they realized they must discover, first of all, what had happened to him and where he was.

So Wisk the Fairy transported himself to the bower of the Fairy Queen, which was located deep in the heart of the Forest of Burzee; and once there, it did not take him long to find out all about the naughty Daemons and how they had kidnapped the good Santa Claus to prevent his making children happy. The Fairy Queen also promised her assistance, and then, fortified by this powerful support, Wisk flew back to where Nuter and Peter and Kilter awaited him, and the four counseled together and laid plans to rescue their master from his enemies.

It is possible that Santa Claus was not as merry as usual during the night that succeeded his capture. For although he had faith in the judgment of his little friends he could not avoid a certain amount of worry, and an anxious look would creep at times into his kind old eyes as he thought of the disappointment that might await his dear little children. And the Daemons, who guarded him by turns, one after another, did not neglect to taunt him with contemptuous words in his helpless condition.

When Christmas Day dawned the Daemon of Malice was guarding the prisoner, and his tongue was sharper than that of any of the others.

"The children are waking up, Santa!" he cried; "they are waking up to find their stockings empty! Ho, ho! How they will quarrel, and wail, and stamp their feet in anger! Our caves will be full today, old Santa! Our caves are sure to be full!"

But to this, as to other like taunts, Santa Claus answered nothing. He was much grieved by his capture, it is true; but his courage did not forsake him. And, finding that the prisoner would not reply to his jeers, the Daemon of Malice presently went away, and sent the Daemon of Repentance to take his place.

This last personage was not so disagreeable as the others. He had gentle and refined features, and his voice was soft and pleasant in tone.

"My brother Daemons do not trust me overmuch," said he, as he entered the cavern; "but it is morning, now, and the mischief is done. You cannot visit the children again for another year."

"That is true," answered Santa Claus, almost cheerfully; "Christmas Eve is past, and for the first time in centuries I have not visited my children."

"The little ones will be greatly disappointed," murmured the Daemon of Repentance, almost regretfully, "but that cannot be helped now. Their grief is likely to make the children selfish and envious and hateful, and if they come to the Caves of the Daemons today I shall lead some of them to my Cave of Repentance."

"Do you never repent, yourself?" asked Santa Claus.

The best gift is the one we ourselves should like most to have. Children in their kindness grant this gift to adults.

"Oh, yes, indeed," answered the Daemon. "I am even now repenting that I assisted in your capture. Of course it is too late to remedy the evil that has been done; but repentance, you know, can come only after an evil thought or deed, for in the beginning there is nothing to repent of."

"So I understand," said Santa Claus. "Those who avoid evil need never visit your cave."

"As a rule, that is true," replied the Daemon; "yet you, who have done no evil, are about to visit my cave at once; for to prove that I sincerely regret my share in your capture I am going to permit you to escape."

This speech greatly surprised the prisoner, until he reflected that it was just what might be expected of the Daemon of Repentance. The fellow at once busied himself untying the knots that bound Santa Claus and unlocking the chains that fastened him to the wall. Then he led the way through a long tunnel until they both emerged in the Cave of Repentance.

"I hope you will forgive me," said the Daemon, pleadingly. "I am not really a bad person, you know; and I believe I accomplish a great deal of good in the world."

With this he opened a back door that let in a flood of sunshine, and Santa Claus sniffed the fresh air gratefully.

"I bear no malice," said he to the Daemon, in a gentle voice; "and I am sure the world would be a dreary place without you. So, good morning, and a Merry Christmas to you!"

With these words he stepped out to greet the bright morning, and a moment later he was trudging along, whistling softly to himself, on his way to his home in the Laughing Valley.

Marching over the snow toward the mountain was a vast army, made up of the most curious creatures imaginable. There were numberless knooks from the forest, as rough and crooked in appearance as the gnarled branches of the trees they ministered to. And there were dainty ryls from the fields, each one bearing the emblem of the flower or plant it guarded. Behind these were many ranks of pixies, gnomes and nymphs, and in the rear a thousand beautiful fairies floating along, all in gorgeous array.

This wonderful army was led by Wisk, Peter, Nuter and Kilter, who had assembled it to rescue Santa Claus from captivity and to punish the Daemons.

But lo! coming to meet his loyal friends appeared the imposing form of Santa Claus, his white beard floating in the breeze and his bright eyes sparkling with pleasure at this proof of the love and veneration he had inspired in the hearts of the most powerful creatures in existence.

And while they clustered around him and danced with glee at his safe return, he gave them earnest thanks for their support. But Wisk, and Nuter, and Peter, and Kilter, he embraced affectionately.

"It is useless to pursue the Daemons," said Santa Claus to the army. "They have their place in the world, and can never be destroyed. But that is a great pity, nevertheless," he continued, musingly.

So the fairies, and knooks, and pixies, and ryls all escorted the good man to his castle, and there left him to talk over the events of the night with his little assistants.

Wisk had already rendered himself invisible and flown through the big world to see how the children were getting along on this bright Christmas morning; and by the time he returned, Peter had finished telling Santa Claus of how they had distributed the toys.

"We really did very well," cried the fairy, in a pleased voice; "for I found little unhappiness among the children this morning. Still, you must not get captured again, my dear master, for we might not be so fortunate another time in carrying out your ideas."

He then related the mistakes that had been made, and which he had not discovered until his tour of inspection. And Santa Claus at once sent him with rubber boots for Charlie Smith, and a doll for Mamie Brown; so that even those two disappointed ones became happy.

As for the wicked Daemons of the Caves, they were filled with anger and chagrin when they found that their clever capture of Santa Claus had come to naught. Indeed, no one on that Christmas Day appeared to be at all selfish, or envious, or hateful. And, realizing that while the children's saint had so many powerful friends it was folly to oppose him, the Daemons never again attempted to interfere with his journeys on Christmas Eve.

Toys, mirror images of our imagination, puppets of our fantasies, are ever "educational" if they make us feel secure and joyful.

Laura Ingalls Wilder

Christmas on the Prairie

The days were short and cold, the wind whistled sharply, but there was no snow. Cold rains were falling. Day after day the rain fell, pattering on the roof and pouring from the eaves.

Mary and Laura stayed close by the fire, sewing their nine-patch quilt blocks, or cutting paper dolls from scraps of wrapping paper, and hearing the wet sound of the rain. Every night was so cold that they expected to see snow next morning, but in the morning they saw only sad, wet grass.

They pressed their noses against the squares of glass in the windows that Pa had made, and they were glad they could see out. But they wished they could see snow.

Laura was anxious because Christmas was near, and Santa Claus and his reindeer could not travel without snow. Mary was afraid that, even if it snowed, Santa Claus could not find them, so far away in Indian Territory. When they asked Ma about this, she said she didn't know.

"What day is it?" they asked her, anxiously. "How many more days till Christmas?" And they counted off the days on their fingers, till there was only one more day left.

Rain was still falling that morning. There was not one crack in the gray sky. They felt almost sure there would be no Christmas. Still, they kept hoping.

Just before noon the light changed. The clouds broke and drifted apart, shining white in a clear blue sky. The sun shone, birds sang, and thousands of drops of water sparkled on the grasses. But when Ma opened the door to let in the fresh, cold air, they heard the creek roaring.

They had not thought about the creek. Now they knew they would have no Christmas, because Santa Claus could not cross that roaring creek.

Pa came in, bringing a big fat turkey. If it weighed less than twenty pounds, he said, he'd eat it, feathers and all. He asked Laura, "How's that for a Christmas dinner? Think you can manage one of those drumsticks?"

She said, yes, she could. But she was sober. Then Mary asked him if the creek was going down, and he said it was still rising.

Ma said it was too bad. She hated to think of Mr. Edwards eating his bachelor cooking all alone on Christmas day. Mr. Edwards had been asked to eat Christmas dinner with them, but Pa shook his head and said a man would risk his neck, trying to cross that creek now.

"No," he said. "That current's too strong. We'll just have to make up our minds that Edwards won't be here tomorrow."

Of course that meant that Santa Claus could not come, either.

Laura and Mary tried not to mind too much. They watched Ma dress the wild turkey, and it was a very fat turkey. They were lucky little girls, to have a good house to live in, and a warm fire to sit by, and such a turkey for their Christmas dinner. Ma said so, and it was true. Ma said it was too bad that Santa Claus couldn't come this year, but they were such good girls that he hadn't forgotten them; he would surely come next year.

Still, they were not happy.

After supper that night they washed their hands and faces, buttoned their red flannel nightgowns, tied their nightcap strings, and soberly said their prayers. They lay down in bed and pulled the covers up. It did not seem at all like Christmastime.

Pa and Ma sat silent by the fire. After a while Ma asked why Pa didn't play the fiddle, and he said, "I don't seem to have the heart to, Caroline."

After a longer while, Ma suddenly stood up.

"I'm going to hang up your stockings, girls," she said. "Maybe something will happen."

Laura's heart jumped. But then she thought again of the creek and she knew nothing could happen.

Ma took one of Mary's clean stockings and one of Laura's, and she hung them from the mantel-shelf, on either side of the fireplace. Laura and Mary watched her over the edge of their bedcovers.

"Now go to sleep," Ma said, kissing them good night. "Morning will come quicker if you're asleep."

She sat down again by the fire and Laura almost went to sleep. She woke up a little when she heard Pa say, "You've only made it worse, Caroline." And she thought she heard Ma say: "No, Charles. There's the white sugar." But perhaps she was dreaming.

The waiting is intolerable; sleep comes sometimes before Santa. Only the most perfect vision is rewarded with a sight of him.

71

Then she heard Jack growl savagely. The door latch rattled and someone said, "Ingalls! Ingalls!" Pa was stirring up the fire, and when he opened the door Laura saw that it was morning. The outdoors was gray.

"Great fishhooks, Edwards! Come in, man! What's happened?" Pa exclaimed.

Laura saw the stockings limply dangling, and she scrooged her shut eyes into the pillow. She heard Pa piling wood on the fire, and she heard Mr. Edwards say he had carried his clothes on his head when he swam the creek. His teeth rattled and his voice shivered. He would be all right, he said, as soon as he got warm.

"It was too big a risk, Edwards," Pa said. "We're glad you're here, but that was too big a risk for a Christmas dinner."

"Your little ones had to have a Christmas," Mr. Edwards replied. "No creek could stop me, after I fetched them their gifts from Independence."

Laura sat straight up in bed. "Did you see Santa Claus?" she shouted.

"I sure did," Mr. Edwards said.

"Where? When? What did he look like? What did he say? Did he really give you something for us?" Mary and Laura cried.

"Wait, wait a minute!" Mr. Edwards laughed. And Ma said she would put the presents in the stockings, as Santa Claus intended. She said they mustn't look.

Mr. Edwards came and sat on the floor by their bed, and he answered every question they asked him. They honestly tried not to look at Ma, and they didn't quite see what she was doing.

When he saw the creek rising, Mr. Edwards said, he had known that Santa Claus could not get across it. ("But you crossed it," Laura said. "Yes," Mr. Edwards replied, "but Santa Claus is too old and fat. He couldn't make it, where a long, lean razorback like me could do so.") And Mr. Edwards reasoned that if Santa Claus couldn't cross the creek, likely he would come no farther south than Independence. Why should he come forty miles across the prairie, only to be turned back? Of course he wouldn't do that!

So Mr. Edwards had walked to Independence. ("In

the rain?" Mary asked. Mr. Edwards said he wore his rubber coat.) And there, coming down the street in Independence, he had met Santa Claus. ("In the daytime?" Laura asked. She hadn't thought that anyone could see Santa Claus in the daytime. No, Mr. Edwards said; it was night, but light shone out across the street from the saloons.)

Well, the first thing Santa Claus said was "Hello, Edwards!" ("Did he know you?" Mary asked, and Laura asked, "How did you know he was really Santa Claus?" Mr. Edwards said that Santa Claus knew everybody. And he had recognized Santa at once by his whiskers. Santa Claus had the longest, thickest, whitest set of whiskers west of the Mississippi.)

So Santa Claus said, "Hello, Edwards! Last time I saw you you were sleeping on a corn-shuck bed in Tennessee." And Mr. Edwards well remembered the little pair of red yarn mittens that Santa Claus had left for him that time.

Then Santa Claus said: "I understand you're living now down along the Verdigris River. Have you ever met up, down yonder, with two little young girls named Mary and Laura?"

"I surely am acquainted with them," Mr. Edwards replied.

"It rests heavy on my mind," said Santa Claus. "They are both of them sweet, pretty, good little young things, and I know they are expecting me. I surely do hate to disappoint two good little girls like them. Yet with the water up the way it is, I can't ever make it across that creek. I can figure no way whatsoever to get to their cabin this year. Edwards," Santa Claus said. "Would you do me the favor to fetch them their gifts this one time?"

"I'll do that, and with pleasure," Mr. Edwards told him.

Then Santa Claus and Mr. Edwards stepped across the street to the hitching posts where the pack mule was tied. ("Didn't he have his reindeer?" Laura asked. "You know he couldn't," Mary said. "There isn't any snow." Exactly, said Mr. Edwards. Santa Claus traveled with a pack mule in the southwest.)

And Santa Claus uncinched the pack and looked

"How did you know he was really Santa Claus?" Laura asked. Mr. Edwards explained he had known Santa at once, by his whiskers.

by packhorse, not reindeer, in the Southwest.

Poem from a King's Prayerbook

In the mid-sixteenth century this poem was written on the flyleaf of a prayerbook belonging to Edward VI, the frail and devout son of Henry VIII who became King of England at nine and died at sixteen. The legend it preserves gives a clue as to how the big bird, long regarded as a bringer of good fortune to the houses on which it nests, became also the bringer of babies.

THE STORK

The stork she rose on Christmas Eve
And said unto her brood,
I now must fare to Bethlehem
To view the Son of God.

She gave to each his dole of meat,
She stowed them fairly in,
And fair she flew and fast she flew
And came to Bethlehem.

The white stork is rare today, its European habitat destroyed.

Now where is He of David's line?
She asked at house and hall.
He is not here, they spake hardly,
But in the manger stall.

She found him in the manger stall
With that most Holy Maid;
The gentle stork she wept to see
The Lord so rudely laid.

Then from her panting breast she plucked
The feathers white and warm;
She strewed them in the manger bed
To keep the Lord from harm.

"Blessed be the gentle stork
Forever more," quoth He,
"For that she saw my sad estate
And showed pity.

"Full welcome shall she ever be
In hamlet and in hall,
And called henceforth the Blessed Bird
And friend of babies all."

A precocious scholar, Boy King Edward VI studied Latin, Greek.

Washington Irving

The Christmas Coach

There is nothing in England that exercises a more delightful spell over my imagination than the lingerings of the holiday customs of former times.

Of all the old festivals, however, that of Christmas awakens the strongest and most heartfelt associations. There is a tone of solemn and sacred feeling that blends with our conviviality, and lifts the spirit to a state of hallowed and elevated enjoyment. The services of the church about this season are extremely tender and in-spiring. They dwell on the beautiful story of the origin of our faith, and the pastoral scenes that accompanied its announcement.

It is a beautiful arrangement that this festival, which commemorates the announcement of the religion of peace and love, has been made the season for the gathering together of family connections, and calling back the children of a family who have launched forth in life and wandered, once more to assemble about the hearth.

Norman Rockwell's son served as model for the boy pressing his nose against the coach window in this classic illustration showing travelers

In the course of a December tour in Yorkshire, I rode for some distance in one of the public coaches, on the day preceding Christmas. The coach was crowded, both inside and out, with passengers, who, by their talk, seemed principally bound to the mansions of relations and friends to eat the Christmas dinner. It was loaded also with hampers of game, and baskets and boxes of delicacies and hares hung dangling their long ears about the coachman's box—presents from distant friends for the impending feasts. I had three fine rosy-cheeked schoolboys for my fellow-passengers inside, full of the buxom health and manly spirits which I have observed in the children of this country. They were returning home for the holidays in high glee, and promising themselves a world of enjoyment. It was delightful to hear the gigantic plans of pleasure of the little rogues, and the imprac-

ticable feats they were to perform during their six weeks' emancipation from the abhorred thraldom of book, birch and pedagogue. They were full of anticipations of the meeting with the family and household, down to the very cat and dog; and of the joy they were to give their little sisters by the presents with which their pockets were crammed; but the meeting to which they seemed to look forward with the greatest impatience was with Bantam, which I found to be a pony, and, according to their talk, possessed of more virtues than any steed since the days of Bucephalus. How he could trot! how he could run! and then such leaps as he would take—there was not a hedge in the country that he could not clear.

They were under the particular guardianship of the coachman, to whom, whenever an opportunity present-ed, they addressed a host of questions, and pronounced

coming home for the holidays. It is the same scene Washington Irving described in his account of a Christmas in England around 1820.

him one of the best fellows in the whole world. Indeed, I could not but notice the more than ordinary air of bustle and importance of the coachman, who wore his hat a little on one side, and had a large bunch of Christmas greens stuck in the buttonhole of his coat. He is always a personage full of mighty care and business, and he is particularly so during this season, having so many commissions to execute in consequence of the great interchange of presents.

Perhaps the impending holiday might have given a more than usual animation to the country, for it seemed to me as if everybody was in good looks and good spirits. Game, poultry and other luxuries of the table were in brisk circulation in the villages; the grocers', butchers' and fruiterers' shops were thronged with customers. The housewives were stirring briskly about, putting their dwellings in order; and the glossy branches of holly, with their bright red berries, began to appear at the windows. The scene brought to mind an old writer's account of Christmas preparations:

"Now capons and hens, besides turkeys, geese, and ducks, with beef and mutton—must all die; for in twelve days a multitude of people will not be fed with a little. Now plums and spice, sugar and honey, square it among pies and broth. Now or never must music be in tune, for the youth must dance and sing to get them a heat, while the aged sit by the fire. The country maid leaves half her market, and must be sent again, if she forgets a pack of cards on Christmas Eve. Great is the contention of Holly and Ivy, whether master or dame wears the breeches. Dice and cards benefit the butler; and if the cook do not lack wit, he will sweetly lick his fingers."

Children, parents, merchants all conspire to make the jolly old man—here painted by N.C. Wyeth—a reality in our lives.

Clement C. Moore

A Visit from St. Nicholas

If it weren't for a dignified professor of religion, author of A Compendious Lexicon of the Hebrew Language, Santa might use handcart or packhorse, or even rocket ship, to deliver toys on Christmas Eve. The sleigh that flies, light as thistledown despite its bulky load of toys; the eight reindeer with magical, mysterious names and prancing hoofs—this marvelous mode of transportation was the inspired creation of Dr. Clement C. Moore, who in 1822 wrote a poem for the amusement of his children.

Dr. Moore was a preacher as well as a teacher, and the son of a bishop. Educated at Columbia University, he knew all there was to know about saints including the Dutch saint, Nicholas, whose name stood for generosity and gift-giving. But Dr. Moore was a warmhearted, tolerant, humorous man, and his version of Saint Nicholas owed more to the jolly traditions of the Dutch settlers of New York than to religious history. Legend has it that he started composing the verses while on a trip to market, by sleigh, to buy the Christmas turkey.

His picture of Santa Claus, jolly and plump, with the stub of his pipe in his teeth, may be a description of the Moores' Dutch handyman, Jan Duyckinck.

Once home, Dr. Moore jotted the verses down on paper, and that night, seated before the fireplace, he read them aloud to his family. Dr. and Mrs. Moore were the parents of six children.

One version of the story has it that there was a guest staying with the Moores that year, in their roomy old-fashioned home called Chelsea House (there's now a New York City skyscraper on the site). If so, she was Miss Harriet Butler, daughter of Moore's friend David Butler, who was rector of a church in Troy, New York, and she later gave a handwritten copy of the poem to the editor of the Troy Sentinel. The following Christmas the poem was printed in that newspaper, and readers were as delighted as Dr. Moore's children had been. Five years later, in 1837, the poem appeared with several others by Dr. Moore in The New York Book of Poetry, and in 1844 it appeared as a book for children, with illustrations.

Since then? No one has an accurate count of how many times the poem has appeared in print, or in how many different languages. It is a worldwide favorite, and the reindeer-drawn sleigh that flies through the night-time sky has become a peculiarly American contribution to the lore of Christmas.

'TWAS THE NIGHT BEFORE CHRISTMAS,
    when all through the house
Not a creature was stirring, not even a mouse;
The stockings were hung by the chimney with
    care
In hopes that ST. NICHOLAS soon would be
    there;
The children were nestled all snug in their beds,
While visions of sugar-plums danced through
    their heads;
And Mamma in her 'kerchief, and I in my cap,
Had just settled our brains for a long winter's
    nap—

When out on the lawn there arose such a
    clatter,
I sprang from my bed to see what was the
    matter;
Away to the window I flew like a flash,
Tore open the shutters and threw up the sash.
The moon on the breast of the new-fallen
    snow
Gave the lustre of midday to objects below;
When, what to my wondering eyes should
    appear,
But a miniature sleigh, and eight tiny reindeer,
With a little old driver, so lively and quick,
I knew in a moment it must be SAINT NICK.
More rapid than eagles his coursers they came,
And he whistled, and shouted, and called them
    by name:

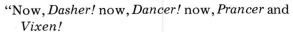

"Now, *Dasher!* now, *Dancer!* now, *Prancer* and
    Vixen!
On, *Comet!* on, *Cupid!* on, *Donder* and *Blitzen!*
To the top of the porch! to the top of the wall!
Now, dash away! dash away! dash away all!"
As dry leaves that before the wild hurricane fly,
When they meet with an obstacle, mount to the sky,

So up to the house-top the coursers they flew,
With a sleigh full of toys—and ST. NICHOLAS too!
And then, in a twinkling, I heard on the roof,
The prancing and pawing of each little hoof.
As I drew in my head, and was turning around
Down the chimney ST. NICHOLAS came with a bound.
He was dressed all in fur, from his head to his foot,
And his clothes were all tarnished with ashes and
    soot!
A bundle of toys he had flung on his back,
And he looked like a pedlar just opening his pack;

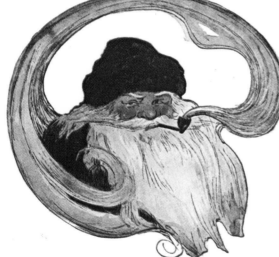

He spoke not a word, but went straight to his work,
And filled all the stockings—then turned with a jerk,
And laying his finger aside of his nose,
And giving a nod, up the chimney he rose.
He sprang to his sleigh, to his team gave a whistle,
And away they all flew, like the down off a thistle.
But I heard him exclaim, ere he drove out of sight,
*"HAPPY CHRISTMAS TO ALL! AND TO ALL
    A GOOD NIGHT!"*

His eyes—how they twinkled! his dimples,
    how merry!
His cheeks were like roses, his nose like a cherry!
His droll little mouth was drawn up like a bow,
And the beard of his chin was as white as the snow.
The stump of a pipe he held tight in his teeth,
And the smoke, it encircled his head like a wreath.
He had a broad face, and a little round belly,
That shook, when he laugh'd, like a bowlful of jelly.
He was chubby and plump; a right jolly old elf;
And I laughed, when I saw him, in spite of myself.
A wink of his eye, and a twist of his head,
Soon gave me to know I had nothing to dread.

Mark Twain

Susie's Letter from Santa

Lucky little Susie Clemens! She lived at 351 Farmington Avenue, Hartford, Connecticut, in the new house that was so much admired by neighbors and townspeople in the 1870's. It was trimmed with shiny red-and-black brickwork; it had three turrets, five balconies, and a forest of chimneys rising from the tile roof. Inside were nineteen large rooms and five bathrooms—in a day when few homes had even one.

Susie lived there with her famous father who wrote and lectured as Mark Twain, though his real name was Samuel Clemens. There were also two younger sisters, a beautiful but delicate mother, and the six servants it took to make

Mark with daughters Susie and Clara.

the huge house livable, but a very special relationship existed between Susie and her father. He treated her like a princess, buying her toys like a silver thimble and a Noah's Ark set that included 200 hand-carved wooden animals. Tragically, Susie died of meningitis when she was only twenty-four. Her brokenhearted father said later that it made him feel a little better to know that she died at home, in the wonderful fairy-tale house where she had spent a happy childhood.

Wonderful Christmases were part and parcel of that happy childhood. One year when she was very young Susie wrote a letter to Santa Claus and received the following letter in reply:

Palace of St. Nicholas
In the Moon
Christmas Morning

My dear Susie Clemens:

I have received and read all the letters which you and your little sister have written me by the hand of your mother and your nurses; I have also read those which you little people have written me with your own hands—for although you did not use any characters that are in grown people's alphabet, you used the characters that all children in all lands on earth and in the twinkling stars use; and as all my subjects in the moon are children and use no character but that, you will easily understand that I can read your and your baby sister's jagged and fantastic marks without any trouble at all. But I had trouble with those letters which you dictated through your mother and the nurses, for I am a foreigner and cannot read English writing well. You will find that I made no mistakes about the things which you and the baby ordered in your own letters—I went down your chimney at midnight when you were asleep and delivered them all myself—and kissed both of you, too, because you are

good children, well trained, nice mannered, and about the most obedient little people I ever saw. But in the letter which you dictated there were some words which I could not make out for certain, and one or two small orders which I could not fill because we ran out of stock. Our last lot of kitchen furniture for dolls has just gone to a very poor little child in the North Star away up in the cold country above the Big Dipper. Your mama can show you that star and you will say: "Little Snow Flake" (for that is the child's name), "I'm glad you got that furniture, for you need it more than I." That is, you must *write* that, with your own hand, and Snow Flake will write you an answer. If you only spoke it she wouldn't hear you. Make your letter light and thin, for the distance is great and the postage very heavy.

There was a word or two in your mama's letter which I couldn't be certain of. I took it to be "a trunk full of doll's clothes." Is that it? I will call at your kitchen door about nine o'clock this morning to inquire. But I must not see anybody and I must not speak to anybody but you. When the kitchen doorbell rings, George must be blindfolded and sent to open the door. Then he must go back to the dining room or the china closet and take the cook with him. You must tell George he must walk on tiptoe and not speak—otherwise he will die someday. Then you must go up to the nursery and stand on a chair or the nurse's bed and put your ear to the speaking tube that leads down to the kitchen and when I whistle through it you must speak in the tube and say, "Welcome, Santa Claus!" Then I will ask whether it was a trunk you ordered or not. If you say it was, I shall ask you what *color* you want the trunk to be. Your mama will help you to name a nice color and then you must tell me every single thing in detail which you want the trunk to contain. Then when I say "Good-bye and a merry Christmas to my little Susie Clemens," you must say "Good-bye, good old Santa Claus, I thank you very much and please tell that little Snow Flake I will look at her star tonight and she must look down here—I will be right in the west bay window; and every fine night I will look at her star and say, 'I know somebody up there and *like* her, too.'" Then you must go down into the library and make George close the doors that open into the main hall and everybody must keep still for a little while. Then while you are waiting I will go to the moon and get those things and in a few minutes I will come down the chimney that belongs to the fireplace that is in the hall—if it is a trunk you want—because I couldn't get such a large thing as a trunk down the nursery chimney, you know.

People may talk if they want, till they hear my footsteps in the hall. Then you tell them to keep quiet a little while until I go up the chimney. Maybe you will not hear my footsteps at all—so you may go now and then and peep through the dining-room doors, and by and by you will see that which you want, right under the piano in the drawing room—for I shall put it there. If I should leave any snow in the hall, you must tell George to sweep it into the fireplace, for I haven't time to do such things. George must not use a broom, but a rag—or he will die someday. You watch George and don't let him run into danger. If my boot should leave a stain on the marble, George must not holystone it away. Leave it there always in memory of my visit; and whenever you look at it or show it to anybody you must let it remind you to be a good little girl. Whenever you are naughty and somebody points to that mark which your good old Santa Claus's boot made on the marble, what will you say, little sweetheart?

Good-bye for a few minutes, till I come down and ring the kitchen doorbell.

Your loving Santa Claus
Whom people sometimes call
"The Man in the Moon"

The young place infinite faith in the mails, dreaming of a snowy Pony Express between their hearth and the frozen tip-top of the world.

Francis P. Church

Yes, Virginia, There is a Santa

Her whole name was Mrs. Laura Virginia O'Hanlon Douglas. She earned a master's degree from Columbia University and a doctorate from Fordham, and she had a long and distinguished career as a teacher and administrator in the New York City school system, but to millions she will always be the little girl who wrote a letter asking about Santa Claus.

"I was only a child, and my parents did everything for me that any parents could do," Mrs. Douglas told an audience of college students some forty years later. "Quite naturally I believed in Santa Claus, for he had never disappointed me. But like you, I turned to those of my own generation, and so when less fortunate little boys and girls said there wasn't any Santa Claus, I was filled with doubts. I asked my father, and he was a little evasive on the subject.

"It was a habit in our family that whenever any

doubts came up as to how to pronounce a word, or some question of historical fact was in doubt, we wrote to the 'Question and Answer' column in The New York Sun. *Father would always say, "If you see it in* The Sun, *it's so," and that settled the matter.*

" 'Well, I'm just going to write to The Sun *and find out the real truth,' I said to father."*

The editorial was written by Francis Pharcellus Church, a Civil War correspondent for the The New York Times *before he joined* The Sun *as a writer specializing in theological and controversial subjects.*

Mr. Church died in 1906.

The New York Sun *died in 1950.*

Mrs. Douglas died May 13, 1971, at the age of eighty-one.

But little Virginia, her letter, and the answer she received will live forever in America's heart.

Dear Editor: I am 8 years old.

Some of my little friends say there is no Santa Claus.

Papa says "If you see it in *The Sun* it's so."

Please tell me the truth; is there a Santa Claus?

Virginia O'Hanlon

Virginia, your little friends are wrong. They have been affected by the skepticism of a skeptical age. They do not believe except they see. They think that nothing can be which is not comprehensible by their little minds. All minds, Virginia, whether they be men's or children's, are little. In this great universe of ours man is a mere insect, an ant, in his intellect, as compared with the boundless world about him, as measured by the intelligence capable of grasping the whole of truth and knowledge.

Yes, Virginia, there is a Santa Claus. He exists as certainly as love and generosity and devotion exist, and you know that they abound and give to your life its highest beauty and joy. Alas! how dreary would be the

world if there were no Santa Claus! It would be as dreary as if there were no Virginias. There would be no childlike faith then, no poetry, no romance to make tolerable this existence. We should have no enjoyment, except in sense and sight. The eternal light with which childhood fills the world would be extinguished.

Not believe in Santa Claus! You might as well not believe in fairies! You might get your papa to hire men to watch in all the chimneys on Christmas Eve to catch Santa Claus, but even if they did not see Santa Claus coming down, what would that prove? Nobody sees Santa Claus, but that is no sign that there is no Santa Claus. The most real things in the world are those that neither children nor men can see.

No Santa Claus! Thank God, he lives, and he lives forever. A thousand years from now, Virginia, nay, ten times ten thousand years from now, he will continue to make glad the heart of childhood.

from *The New York Sun*, September 21, 1897

People dress up like him, we sing about him, artists paint him. Someone must have seen him, else how would we know just how he looks?

91

No matter the snow, no matter the cold, errands of good cheer and friendship bring everyone out of his house at Christmastime.

Hamlin Garland

My First Christmas Tree

When I was ten years old we moved to Mitchell County, an Iowa prairie land, and there we prospered in such wise that our stockings always held toys of some sort, and even my mother's stocking occasionally sagged with a simple piece of jewelry or a new comb or brush. But the thought of a family tree remained the luxury of millionaire city dwellers; indeed it was not till my fifteenth or sixteenth year that our Sunday school rose to the extravagance of a tree, and it is of this wondrous festival that I write.

The land about us was only partly cultivated at this time, and our district schoolhouse, a bare little box, was set bleakly on the prairie; but the Burr Oak schoolhouse was not only larger but it stood beneath great oaks as well and possessed the charm of a forest background through which a stream ran silently. It was our chief social center. There of a Sunday a regular preacher held "Divine Service" with Sunday school as a sequence. At night—usually on Friday nights—the young people met in "lyceums," as we called them, to debate great questions or to "speak pieces" and read essays; and here it was that I saw my first Christmas tree.

I walked to that tree across four miles of moonlit snow. Snow? No, it was a floor of diamonds, a magical world, so beautiful that my heart still aches with the wonder of it and with the regret that it has all gone—gone with the keen eyes and the bounding pulses of the boy.

Our home at this time was a small frame house on the prairie almost directly west of the Burr Oak grove, and as it was too cold to take the horses out my brother and I, with our tall boots, our visored caps and our long woolen mufflers, started forth afoot, defiant of the cold. We left the gate on the trot, bound for a sight of the glittering unknown. The snow was deep and we moved side by side in the grooves made by the hoofs of the horses, setting our feet in the shine left by the broad shoes of the wood sleighs whose going had smoothed the way for us.

Our breaths rose like smoke in the still air. It must have been ten below zero, but that did not trouble us in those days, and at last we came in sight of the lights, in sound of the singing, the laughter, the bells of the feast.

It was a poor little building without tower or bell and its low walls had but three windows on a side, and yet it seemed very imposing to me that night as I crossed the threshold and faced the strange people who packed it to the door. I say "strange people," for though I had seen most of them many times they all seemed somehow alien to me that night. I was an irregular attendant at Sunday school and did not expect a present; therefore I stood against the wall and gazed with open-eyed marveling at the shining pine which stood where the pulpit was wont to be. I was made to feel the more embarrassed by reason of the remark of a boy who accused me of having forgotten to comb my hair.

This was not true, but the cap I wore always matted my hair down over my brow, and then, when I lifted it off, invariably disarranged it completely. Nevertheless I felt guilty—and hot. I don't suppose my hair was artistically barbered that night—I rather guess Mother had used the shears—and I can believe that I looked the half-wild colt that I was; but there was no call for that youth to direct attention to my unavoidable shagginess.

I don't think the tree had many candles, and I don't remember that it glittered with golden apples. But it was loaded with presents, and the girls coming and going clothed in bright garments made me forget my own looks—I think they made me forget to remove my overcoat, which was a sodden thing of poor cut and worse quality. I think I must have stood agape for nearly two hours listening to the songs, noting every motion of Adoniram Burtch and Asa Walker as they directed the ceremonies and prepared the way for the great event— that is to say, for the coming of Santa Claus himself.

A furious jingling of bells, a loud voice outside, the lifting of a window, the nearer clash of bells, and the dear old Saint appeared (in the person of Stephen Bartle) clothed in a red robe, a belt of sleigh bells, and a long white beard. The children cried out, "Oh!" The girls tittered and shrieked with excitement, and the boys laughed and clapped their hands. Then "Sandy" made a little speech about being glad to see us all, but as he had many other places to visit, and as there were a great many presents to distribute, he guessed he'd have to ask some of the many pretty girls to help him. So he called

From a long way off comes a letter from a friend whose kindness time has not dimmed. You hear from him once a year, less sometimes, but thoughts and best wishes suddenly ring through the cold air with the clarity of a silver bell—yours, and the friend's. Dale Nichols painted the mail sleigh making its rounds. At right, the Christmas tree lives even though it has been cut off from the forest; candles, caught in the constellations of tinsel and angel hair, mirror the stars outside. This seen-through-a-window scene was painted by Stevan Dohanos.

upon Betty Burtch and Hattie Knapp—and I for one admired his taste, for they were the most popular maids of the school.

They came up blushing, and a little bewildered by the blaze of publicity thus blown upon them. But their native dignity asserted itself, and the distribution of the presents began. I have a notion now that the fruit upon the tree was mostly bags of popcorn and "corny copias" of candy, but as my brother and I stood there that night and saw everybody, even the rowdiest boy, getting something we felt aggrieved and rebellious. We forgot that we had come from afar—we only knew that we were being left out.

But suddenly, in the midst of our gloom, my brother's name was called, and a lovely girl with a gentle smile handed him a bag of popcorn. My heart glowed with gratitude. Somebody had thought of us; and when she came to me, saying sweetly, "Here's something for you,"

I had not words to thank her. This happened nearly forty years ago, but her smile, her outstretched hand, her sympathetic eyes are vividly before me as I write. She was sorry for the shock-headed boy who stood against the wall, and her pity made the little box of candy a casket of pearls. The fact that I swallowed the jewels on the road home does not take from the reality of my adoration.

At last I had to take my final glimpse of that wondrous tree, and I well remember the walk home. My brother and I traveled in wordless companionship. The moon was sinking toward the west, and the snow crust gleamed with a million fairy lamps. The sentinel watchdogs barked from lonely farmhouses, and the wolves answered from the ridges. Now and then sleighs passed us with lovers sitting two and two, and the bells on their horses had the remote music of romance to us whose boots drummed like clogs of wood upon the icy road.

Midnight, a country church, a patient horse, the deep and dreamless sleep of the winter solstice, as painted by Mead Schaeffer.

Teddy's eldest daughter, Alice, having persuaded the photographer to include pets, sits with brothers Theodore, Jr., Kermit, Archibald, Quentin, and sister Ethel.

The President poses with his sons in 1904. He adored them; they were integral members of the Cabinet and every safari he took.

Theodore Roosevelt

The Tree in the White House Closet

hy was the Christmas tree in a closet? Because President Theodore Roosevelt had decreed there would be no tree in the White House in 1902. Not that TR was against Christmas. Far from it! The gregarious TR, his gracious wife and his lively brood celebrated the holiday with their customary gusto—as the letter indicates. There were gifts for all, games and sports, memorable meals, parties and dancing. But, in 1902, no tree.

The President was an ardent conservationist second. He was horrified to learn that young pines and spruces had been carelessly cut from some of the national forests, for sale as Christmas trees. He feared that the increasing demand for Christmas trees might ravage the woodlands he loved and valued. Always one to practice what he preached, TR announced that the first family would do without a tree.

TR reckoned without the resourceful sons who got their independence of mind from him. Archie, eight, and Quentin, five, managed to purchase and smuggle into the White House a contraband tree. A sympathetic White House carpenter helped them to erect it in a place where it would be safely out of sight till Christmas morning— inside a closet that opened off the boys' room.

There is a happy footnote to the story. Gifford Pinchot, chief of the U.S. Bureau of Forests and a close friend, managed to persuade TR that some selective cutting of young trees could actually benefit the forests, and before the next Christmas rolled around the ban on White House trees was lifted. About that same time, the U.S. government began to encourage farmers to plant and harvest Christmas trees as a cash crop. This soon provided an adequate supply for the market and pressure on the natural forests was reduced.

Theodore Roosevelt *writes to* Master James A. Garfield

White House, December 26, 1902.
Jimmikins:

. . . . Yesterday morning at a quarter of seven all the children were up and dressed and began to hammer at the door of their mother's and my room, in which their six stockings, all bulging out with queer angles and rotundities, were hanging from the fireplace. So their mother and I got up, shut the window, lit the fire (taking down the stockings, of course), put on our wrappers and prepared to admit the children. But first there was a surprise for me, also for their good mother, for Archie had a little Christmas tree of his own, which he had

The first President to have a Christmas tree in the White House was Franklin Pierce.
The year was 1832, and the guests he invited in to see the lighted and decorated tree
were fellow members of the New York Avenue Presbyterian Church.
Larger and more widely publicized was the White House tree of 1889,
when the Benjamin Harrisons observed the holiday season with warmhearted hospitality.
It is the duty of Christians to make merry, President Harrison proclaimed;
and he is generally regarded as the Chief Executive who set the pattern
for seasonal festivity at 1600 Pennsylvania Avenue.

News stories about Roosevelt sparing the life of a cub while on a bear hunt inspired toy manufacturers to produce the "Teddy."

rigged up with the help of one of the carpenters in a big closet; and we all had to look at the tree and each of us got a present off of it. There was also one present each for Jack, the dog, Tom Quartz, the kitten, and Algonquin, the pony, whom our Archie would no more think of neglecting than I would neglect his brothers and sisters. Then all the children came into our bed and there they opened their stockings. Afterward we got dressed and took breakfast, and then all

went into the library, where each child had a table set for his bigger presents. Quentin had a perfectly delightful electric railroad, which had been rigged up for him by one of his friends, the White House electrician, who has

been very good to all the children. Then Ted and I, with General Wood and Mr. Bob Ferguson, who was a lieutenant in my regiment, went for a three-hour ride; and all of us, including all the children, took lunch at the house with the children's aunt, Mrs. Captain Cowles—Archie and Quentin having their lunch at a little table with their cousin Sheffield. Late

in the afternoon I played games of single stick with General Wood and also Mr. Ferguson. I am going to get your father to come on and try it soon. We have to try to hit as light as possible, but sometimes we hit hard, and today I have a bump over one eye and a swollen wrist. Then all our family and kinsfolk and the Senator and Mrs. Lodge's family and kinsfolk had our Christmas dinner at the White House, and afterward danced in the East Room, closing up with the Virginia reel.

On the morning of December 25th, in full orchestra, the world awakes. Normal two-armed children turn into octopuses as their hands become almost as full as the hearts of grandparents eager to please. What more joyous than dolls and drums, trumpets and toy soldiers?

Dylan Thomas

Conversation about Christmas

Small *Boy:* Years and years ago, when you were a boy . . .

Self: When there were wolves in Wales, and birds the colour of red-flannel petticoats whisked past the harp-shaped hills, when we sang and wallowed all night and day in caves that smelt like Sunday afternoons in damp front farmhouse parlours, and chased, with the jawbones of deacons, the English and the bears . . .

Small Boy: You are not so old as Mr. Beynon Number Twenty-Two who can remember when there were no motors. Years and years ago, when you were a boy . . .

Self: Oh, before the motor even, before the wheel, before the duchess-faced horse, when we rode the daft and happy hills bareback . . .

Small Boy: You're not so daft as Mrs. Griffiths up the street, who says she puts her ear under the water in the reservoir and listens to the fish talk Welsh. When you were a boy, what was Christmas like?

Self: It snowed.

Small Boy: It snowed last year, too. I made a snowman and my brother knocked it down and I knocked my brother down and then we had tea.

Self: But that was not the same snow. Our snow was not only shaken in whitewash buckets down the sky, I think it came shawling out of the ground and swam and drifted out of the arms and hands and bodies of the trees; snow grew overnight on the roofs of the houses like a pure and grandfather moss, minutely ivied the walls, and settled on the postman, opening the gate, like a dumb, numb thunderstorm of white, torn Christmas cards.

Small Boy: Were there postmen, then, too?

Self: With sprinkling eyes and wind-cherried noses, on spread, frozen feet they crunched up to the doors and mittened on them manfully. But all that the children could hear was a ringing of bells.

Small Boy: You mean that the postman went rat-a-tat-tat and the doors rang?

Self: The bells that the children could hear were inside them.

Small Boy: I hear thunder sometimes, never bells.

Self: There were church bells, too.

Small Boy: Inside them?

Self: No, no, no, in the bat-black, snow-white belfries, tugged by bishops and storks. And they rang their tidings over the bandaged town, over the frozen foam of the powder and ice-cream hills, over the crackling sea. It seemed that all the churches boomed, for joy, under my window; and the weathercocks crew for Christmas, on our fence.

Small Boy: Get back to the postmen.

Self: They were just ordinary postmen, fond of walking, and dogs, and Christmas, and the snow. They knocked on the doors with blue knuckles . . .

"These wait all upon thee; that thou mayest give them their meat in due season."

Psalms 104:27

CHARLES LIVINGSTON BULL

His aching back, his dog nipped shins, his cold reddened nose belie the satisfaction he gets from delivering happiness to his constituents.

Small Boy: Ours has got a black knocker . . .

Self: And then they stood on the white welcome mat in the little, drifted porches, and clapped their hands together, and huffed and puffed, making ghosts with their breath, and jogged from foot to foot like small boys wanting to go out.

Small Boy: And then the Presents?

Self: And then the Presents, after the Christmas box. And the cold postman, with a rose on his button-nose, tingled down the teatray-slithered run of the chilly glinting hill. He went in his ice-bound boots like a man on fishmonger's slabs. He wagged his bag like a frozen camel's hump, dizzily turned the corner on one foot, and, by God, he was gone.

Small Boy: Get back to the Presents.

Self: There were the Useful Presents: engulfing mufflers of the old coach days, and mittens made for giant sloths; zebra scarves of a substance like silky gum that could be tug-o'-warred down to the galoshes; blinding tam-o'-shanters like patchwork tea-cosies, and bunny-scutted busbies and balaclavas for victims of head-shrinking tribes; from aunts who always wore wool next to the skin, there were moustached and rasping vests that made you wonder why the aunties had any skin left at all; and once I had a little crocheted nosebag from an aunt now, alas, no longer whinnying with us. And pictureless books in which small boys, though warned, with quotations, not to, *would* skate on Farmer Garge's pond, and did, and drowned; and books that told me everything about the wasp, except why.

Small Boy: Get on to the Useless Presents.

Self: On Christmas Eve I hung at the foot of my bed Bessie Bunter's black stocking, and always, I said, I would stay awake all the moonlit, snowlit night to hear the roof-alighting reindeer and see the hollied boot descend through soot. But soon the sand of the snow drifted into my eyes, and though I stared towards the fireplace and around the flickering room where the black sacklike stocking hung, I was asleep before the chimney trembled and the room was red and white with Christmas. But in the morning, though no snow melted on the bedroom floor, the stocking bulged and brimmed: press it, it squeaked like a mouse-in-a-box; it smelt of tangerine; a furry arm lolled over, like the arm of a kangaroo out of its mother's belly; squeeze it hard in the middle, and something squelched; squeeze it again—squelch again. Look out of the frost-scribbled window: on the great loneliness of the small hill, a blackbird was silent in the snow.

Small Boy: Were there any sweets?

Self: Of course there were sweets. It was the marshmallows that squelched. Hardboileds, toffee, fudge and allsorts, crunches, cracknels, humbugs, glaciers, and marzipan and butterwelsh for the Welsh. And troops of bright tin soldiers who, if they would not fight, could always run. And Snakes-and-Families and Happy Ladders. And Easy Hobbi-Games for Little Engineers, complete with Instructions. Oh, easy for Leonardo! And a whistle to make the dogs bark to wake up the old man next door to make him beat on the wall with his stick to shake our picture off the wall. And a packet of cigarettes: you put one in your mouth and you stood at the corner of the street and you waited for hours, in vain, for an old lady to scold you for smoking a cigarette and then, with a smirk, you ate it. And, last of all, in the toe of the stocking, sixpence like a silver corn. And then downstairs for breakfast under the balloons!

Small Boy: Were there Uncles, like in our house?

Self: There are always Uncles at Christmas. The same Uncles. And on Christmas mornings, with dog-disturbing whistle and sugar fags, I would scour the swathed town for the news of the little world, and find always a dead bird by the white Bank or by the deserted swings: perhaps a robin, all but one of his fires out, and that fire still burning on his breast. Men and women wading and scooping back from church or chapel, with taproom noses and wind-smacked cheeks, all albinos, huddled their stiff black jarring feathers against the irreligious snow. Mistletoe hung from the gas in all the front parlours; there was sherry and walnuts and bottled beer and crackers by the dessertspoons; and cats in their fur-abouts watched the fires; and the high-heaped fires crackled and spat, all ready for the chestnuts and the mulling pokers. Some few large men sat in the front

Norman Rockwell used a favorite model, James K. Van Brunt, a man! for all three of these gossiping aunts.

parlours, without their collars, Uncles almost certainly, trying their new cigars, holding them out judiciously at arm's-length, returning them to their mouths, coughing, then holding them out again as though waiting for the explosion; and some few small aunts, not wanted in the kitchen, nor anywhere else for that matter, sat on the very edges of their chairs, poised and brittle, afraid to break, like faded cups and saucers. Not many those mornings trod the piling streets: an old man always, fawn-bowlered, yellow-gloved, and, at this time of year, with spats of snow, would take his constitutional to the white bowling-green, and back, as he would take it wet or fine on Christmas Day or Doomsday. . . .

Small Boy: Why didn't you go home for Christmas dinner?

Self: Oh, but I did, I always did. I would be slap-dashing home, the gravy smell of the dinners of others, the bird smell, the brandy, the pudding and mince, weaving up my nostrils, when out of a snow-clogged side-lane would come a boy the spit of myself, with a pink-tipped cigarette and the violet past of a black eye, cocky as a bullfinch, leering all to himself. I hated him on sight and sound, and would be about to put my dog-whistle to my lips and blow him off the face of Christmas when suddenly he, with a violent wink, put *his* whistle to *his* lips and blew so stridently, so high, so exquisitely loud, that gobbling faces, their cheeks bulged with goose, would press against their tinseled windows, the whole length of the white echoing street.

Small Boy: What did you have for Dinner?

Self: Turkey, and blazing pudding.

Small Boy: Was it nice?

Self: It was not made on earth.

Small Boy: What did you do after dinner?

Self: The Uncles sat in front of the fire, took off their collars, loosened all buttons, put their large moist hands over their watchchains, groaned a little, and slept. Mothers, aunts, and sisters scuttled to and fro, bearing tureens. The dog was sick. Auntie Beattie had to have three aspirins, but Auntie Hannah, who liked port, stood in the middle of the snowbound backyard, singing like a big-bosomed thrush. I would blow up balloons to see how big they would blow up to; and, when they burst, which they all did, the Uncles jumped and rumbled. In the rich and heavy afternoon, the Uncles breathing like dolphins and the snow descending, I would sit in the front room, among festoons and Chinese lanterns, and nibble at dates, and try to make a model man-o'-war, following the Instructions for Little Engineers, and produce what might be mistaken for a seagoing tram. And then, at Christmas tea, the recovered Uncles would be jolly over their mince-pies; and the great iced cake loomed in the centre of the table like a marble grave. Auntie Hannah laced her tea with rum, because it was only once a year. And in the evening, there was Music. An uncle played the fiddle, a cousin sang Cherry Ripe, and another uncle sang Drake's Drum. It was very warm in the little house. Auntie Hannah, who had got on to the parsnip wine, sang a song about Rejected Love, and Bleeding Hearts, and Death, and then another in which she said that her Heart was like a Bird's Nest; and then everybody laughed again, and then I went to bed. Looking through my bedroom window, out into the moonlight and the flying, unending, smoke-coloured snow, I could see the lights in the windows of all the other houses on our hill, and hear the music rising from them up the long, steadily falling night. I turned the gas down, I got into bed. I said some words to the close and holy darkness, and then I slept.

Small Boy: But it all sounds just like an ordinary Christmas.

Self: It was.

Small Boy: But Christmas when you were a boy wasn't any different to Christmas now.

Self: It was, it was.

Small Boy: Why was Christmas different then?

Self: I mustn't tell you.

Small Boy: Why mustn't you tell me? Why is Christmas different for me?

Self: I mustn't tell you.

Small Boy: Why can't Christmas be the same for me as it was for you when you were a boy?

Self: I mustn't tell you. I mustn't tell you because it is Christmas now.

Against the white paper of time we cut our own silhouettes. Christmas is the moment we take the impression,   discord or content.

J. W. Foley

Tommy's Letters

Appletown, December 1, 1905.

Dear Grandma:

I have often thought of you in the past year but you know how busy boys have to be to keep all the chores done and go to school. We do not get much time to write letters. But the other day I was thinking how kind you had always been to us boys and it was a shame I do not write oftener. So today I sat right down after I came from school to write you a good, long letter and let you know that I often think of you even if I do not write. The ground here is all white with snow which makes us think that it will soon be Christmas again. I suppose you do not care so much for Christmas now as you did when you were a little girl. Mamma says that after folks grow up they do not care so much for it except to make the boys and girls happy by giving them something that they want. It must be awful nice to send a sled or a pair of skates or a tool chest to a boy and then sit on Christmas day and think how happy he is. If all of us did that what a bright world it would be. I suppose though that when folks grow up they have so very many things to think about they forget to send things, when they mean to send them all the time but it slips their mind. It isn't that they can't afford it or don't want to but they don't just happen to think about it until it's Christmas day and then it is too late. And then they must feel awful

sorry to think how happy it would have made some little boy if they had sent something but they didn't.

I have an idea Eddie Brooks' Grandma is going to send him a sled for Christmas. I don't know what makes me think so, but it seems to me I heard it somewhere. I guess I can make my old one do for another year. One of the runners is broke but I think I can get it fixed. It won't be very safe though.

Dear Grandma, I hope you are having a good winter and your rheumatism don't bother you very much. I often wish I was there to carry out ashes for you and do the heavy work but I have to go to school so I will grow up and be a credit to you all. You know I am named after Grandpa, which makes me all the more anxious to grow up well.

With much love from us all,

Your affectionate grandson,
Tommy

Appletown, December 1, 1905.

Dear Uncle Bill:

I guess you will be surprised when you get this letter because you don't expect any from me but I was writing to Grandma today and I thought I would write to all of our folks and let them know how I am getting along. You know boys don't write very much because they write compositions in school and that takes about all the time they have got to spare for writing. But we ought to write to our relatives once in a while because we are apt to grow up and go away and then the family will be all broke up and scattered. I know you are a bachelor and haven't got any boys to call your own and that maybe it will interest you to know that I'm getting along

Mischief disappears. In its place wings sprout, rooms tidy, slippers and pipes arrive; briefly father and mother are boss.

very well in school because I am your nephew on my mother's side.

It don't seem like over a year since you sent me my pair of skates for Christmas, does it? I wonder if you have changed very much. I have, a good deal. I am tall and my feet are bigger and the skates you sent me are hardly big enough for me now but I guess I can make them do through the winter. One of the straps is wore out but I guess I can have it fixed so it will do. It is quite dangerous to skate with old straps on, though. One of the boys slipped last week and nearly went into an air hole. His skates were too small and one of the straps broke and let him slide.

We ought to be glad of what we have, though, and not expect new skates every year when we are growing so fast.

I suppose you are too busy to think much about Christmas. I enclose you a copy of a letter I wrote to Santa Claus telling what I want. Of course I know all about who Santa Claus is, but I only send it to show you how well I am getting along in writing and spelling. I think Grandmamma is apt to send me the sled and Papa said if I would be a good boy he would get me the tool chest. So that only leaves the skates and if I don't get a new pair the old ones will do.

I hope you are having good health. I wish I could be where I could help you sometimes in your office, cleaning out the wastebasket and doing the sweeping which I would be only too glad to do if we both lived in the same town. We all send our best love to you.

Your affectionate nephew,
Tommy

Appletown, December 1, 1905.

Dear Aunt Lizzie:

Maybe you have almost forgotten about your little nephew Tommy away out here and so I thought I would drop you a few lines to let you know I am well and getting along fine and hope you are the same. I do not write letters very often because you know how it is with boys. They cannot think of many things to say and are apt to make a good many blots if they write with ink. I just happened to think that maybe I had never written to thank you for those splendid books you sent me for last Christmas and as Christmas will soon be here again I do not want to get too far behind. They were splendid books and I have read them all over and over again. I do not know of anything a boy likes better than books. It improves the mind and keeps them out of mischief and when we grow up to be men we can look back and see how the good books we got for Christmas helped to make us better. Nobody ever regrets sending a boy good books for Christmas, don't you think so?

One of the books you sent me had a sequel. It was the Red Ranger or the Mystery of the Indian Scout. The sequel is the Lost Trail or the Lives of the Gold-Hunters. We do not have it in the bookstore here. I am awful anxious to know if the Red Ranger finds the Lost Trail or not. Have you ever read the sequel? If you have I wish you would write and tell me if he finds the lost trail. I have lent the Red Ranger to some of the boys and they will all appreciate it very much if you will let us know.

If you know any good books for boys I wish you would write down their names and send them to me.

You know two or three good books will last you nearly all winter. Some parts you can read over and over again where there is a lot of excitement until they are nearly worn out. The Red Ranger was that kind and the sequel would probably be almost as good.

It is too bad we are so far away from each other. Sometimes I think how much I could help you and Uncle Jerry not having any boys of your own it would be extremely valuable to you. By chopping wood and filling the woodbox and otherwise doing chores. I could run in on the way from school and see if I couldn't do some chores for you.

I hope you and Uncle Jerry will have a Merry Christmas.

Your affectionate nephew,
Tommy

P.S.—We all send love. The Red Ranger is by the author of the Desert Chief or the Capture of the White Princess.

Tommy

The magnifying glass is only for Santa's eyes; there are good children enough everywhere and Christmas makes them even better.

Donald Culross Peattie

Gold, Frankincense and Myrrh

Beneath the fragrant Christmas tree lie piled the gifts in their gay wrappings. Eager hands reach for them, and the children seize their own with innocent greediness. But in this first glow of the holy morning, before we tear at the bright papers and ribbons, let us pause to remember the meaning of presents on Christmas Day. It is very ancient, as old as the gospel itself. A gift given at Christmastime symbolizes the love that Christians bear to one another, in the name of One who loved them all.

Wise men indeed were they that first intended this, and wise men were the first Christmas givers. Only in St. Matthew's Gospel do we read about them, and he tells it in this wise:

"Now when Jesus was born in Bethlehem of Judea in the days of Herod the king, behold, there came wise men from the east to Jerusalem, saying, Where is he that is born King of the Jews? for we have seen his star in the east, and are come to worship him."

Thus begins the second chapter of Matthew; and later the apostle adds:

"When they saw the star, they rejoiced with exceeding great joy. And when they were come into the house, they saw the young child with Mary his mother, and fell down, and worshipped him: and when they had opened their treasures, they presented unto him gifts; gold, and frankincense, and myrrh."

How strangely scented and melodiously ringing are those three names! All the distant East, all the splendor of kings, the mystery that lies in things faraway and long ago, come to us in those syllables.

Myrrh, and frankincense, and gold! Why were these things chosen? Whence did they come? And what, in actuality, are they?

They are emblems of princely generosity, costly now as in ancient times, and still surviving at many a Christian altar.

The Magi brought their best to the Newborn. They must have felt that nothing poor earth could offer to the King of Heaven would be more appropriate than gold. Well may we agree with them today, for gold is one of the noble metals. No single acid can destroy it, not will it rust away, like iron or tin. As a consequence, it is almost never found as a compound, but in free nuggets or as dust, or alloyed with such metals as mercury or silver. No one can successfully imitate or fake gold, so heavy and incorruptible is it. And it is a metal easily turned to the uses of beauty. It has been woven into fabrics at least since Biblical times (Exodus 39:2-3), for its ductility, as chemists say, is so great that a single grain of fine gold may be drawn out into a wire 1/1000 of an inch in diameter, extending for a length of about one mile.

Pure, supple, almost indestructible, gold is indeed a royal metal among all the base ones occurring in the earth's crust.

The expert hammer of a goldbeater, whose ancient art is referred to by Homer, can beat an ounce of gold into a sheet two hundred feet square, a mere shimmering film. Ordinarily, such beaten gold is made into "books" containing twenty-five leaves apiece, each three and one-quarter inches square. When pure gold becomes this thin, it will transmit light almost like glass, but dimly, letting only the green rays through. With this gold the artist gilds his statue, the bookbinder stamps the title on his fine volume.

In the ancient world into which Christianity was born, gold was far rarer than now; the golden ornaments retrieved by archaeologists from graves in Troy or Crete or Egypt were royal or noble treasures exclusively. Not every wife, then, could wear a precious little band on her fourth finger. But as gold became a medium of exchange, it traveled the world. It came to Palestine from Egyptian Nubia, which we call the northern Sudan; also from the Midianites, who wandered through what is now central Jordan, south and east of the Dead Sea. Where did the Three Wise Men get it? As we are not sure where they themselves came from, we can but guess that—if they truly were "kings of Orient," as the old carols call them—they may have brought their gold from the mines of Indian Mysore.

In any case, it was in love and reverence that the Wise Men offered to the Christ Child the most precious stuff the ancient world knew.

Since those same ancient days, also, many have be-

The commercial treasures of the Middle East honored the birth of Him whose body would in death be anointed by the same spices.

lieved that "incense owns a Deity nigh." No one knows who first lit incense to his God, but doubtless he who did it reasoned that, since all of us enjoy agreeable smells, God probably liked them too. So as times grew less savage and the rituals of worship more spiritualized, burning incense was substituted for the smoke of sacrificial flesh upon the altar. But that sweet reek was not common until the time of Jeremiah. After his day, it was made from an expensive and elaborate formula, containing sixteen different ingredients, with only priests allowed to concoct it. And the chief element in this holy recipe was frankincense, the second gift of the wise men to the Child.

Frankincense is a resin, from a kind of tree held so sacred of old that in southern Arabia and Ethiopia, where it grew, only a few particularly pure persons were allowed even to approach it.

Legends told that the precious trees were guarded by winged serpents. All this makes the tree sound fabulous, but it does indeed exist in Nature, and botanists have named it. It belongs to the genus *Boswellia*, and is a member of the torchwood family. This means little to most of us, unless we happen to have seen the rare elephant trees that grow in the Gila and Imperial valleys in our own far Southwest—the only members of the family native to the continental United States.

To conjure up a frankincense tree, think of a tree about fifteen feet high, with a patchy bark like a sycamore's. It is as crooked as a snake and all but leafless. The few leaves are compound, like those of an ash, and they sprout at the end of the crazy twigs. The flowers and fruit vaguely resemble a cherry's, although this tree is neither sycamore nor ash nor cherry; indeed, the scaly bark and contorted limbs remind one more of some archaic reptile than of the pleasant shady comfort that we call a tree.

To obtain the precious frankincense itself, an Arab cuts a slash in the trunk, as a Vermonter cuts a maple, and then strips off a narrow piece of bark, about five inches long, below the cut. The sap slowly oozes out and is allowed to harden for about three months. At last it is collected in lumps, to be shipped from such strange and faraway places as Berbera and Aden, near the mouth of the Red Sea, and Bombay.

These lumps are yellow or colorless, dusty-looking, with a bitter taste. But they burn with a bright white flame, and then there arises to heaven that sweet, heavy perfume of mystery the Wise Men thought pleasing to God.

This ritual of burning frankincense had been beloved of the Old Testament worshippers long before the night of the Star and the journey of the three wondering Magi toward it in the dark. But Christians did not adopt frankincense till five whole centuries after the Nativity. It is, however, approved for use in the New Testament. Today it finds a place chiefly in the Catholic Church, whose shrines are still full of its perfume. Incense today is compounded partly of the real frankincense and partly of the resin of a very different tree, the spruce fir of northern Europe.

Nowadays the source of true frankincense is not so much Arabia and Ethiopia as the island of Socotra off Africa's eastern tip—a remote, mountainous, harborless island of stones and thorny thickets, where the frankincense trees were, at least until recent times, guarded by the subjects of an Arabian sultan.

From this same distant part of the world comes the last of the gifts of the Magi, myrrh, a shrub related to frankincense, of the genus *Commiphora*. The sap of myrrh is extracted in the same way as that of frankincense, and it comes in small lumps of reddish-brown resin. But its symbolism is more somber. The word myrrh comes from the Hebrew *mar*, meaning "bitter." The ancient Egyptians used this resin in embalming, and hence its connection with solemn occasions. Was this a strange gift for an Infant King? Not for one destined to die for his people.

Such were the first of all Christmas presents, birthday presents to the little Lord of Light. They were offered in a spirit of wondering humility and love.

In all that we ourselves may give, gaily in the modern manner, may there linger too some sweet savor, some hidden glint, of the greater love that gives the celebration of Christmas its real meaning!

Christmas is the birthday of childhood; all people, no matter their ages, are invited to the celebration of this birth.

The crowds are thick, the time is short, the mind works furiously to keep pace with the purse. The list dwindles, disappears. Success!

Irvin S. Cobb

Christmas Gifts—Giving and Getting

To a happily married man the proper exercise of the true Christian spirit consists largely in giving your wife for Christmas the things she wants most and having her give you the things she wants next to most. With scarcely a break the arrangement has come down to us married men from the Garden of Eden. Maybe Christmas wasn't organized then, but woman was. I am indulging in no cheap punnery when I refer to the mother of our race as the First Christmas Eve.

I picture the scene: It is nightfall of December the twenty-fourth in the year One, B.C. The lion and the lamb lie down to rest together. The time is about to come when should these two lie down together only the lion will get up in the morning, the lamb remaining down until thoroughly digested. But now the first vegetarian-ism epidemic is in vogue and there are no meat-eaters. Our original grandparents also seek repose upon the grassy lea. It is by deliberate intent that the lady in the case has lured her guileless helpmate to a spot where the heaviest laden apple tree in the orchard—and the only one in the entire collection bearing a sign reading "All Persons Are Prohibited From Picking Fruit off This Tree"—spreads its sheltering boughs. There is a purpose in the woman's seeming fancy. She knows exactly what she is about. But Adam, the poor slob, suspects nothing. That is the first woman he has ever met. He is, as the saying goes, easy. He prepares to stretch himself beneath the leafy canopy. He aims to drift right off to sleep. He has put in a hard day, loafing round and killing time. Work hasn't been created into the world yet, and the poor, bored wretch is all fagged out from doing nothing. Eve speaks.

"Adam," she says, "tomorrow will be Christmas in the Garden. Let us hang up our fig leaves—Santa Claus might bring us something."

"Where do you get that Santa Claus stuff?" responds Adam, not unkindly, mind you, but in a spirit of gentle raillery. "I'm a grown man," says Adam.

"Are you, really?" she asks. There is a hidden meaning in her bantering reply, but it goes over his head. "Anyhow, dearie, let's hang up our fig leaves—there can't be any harm in it. Just to humor me, now—please!"

"Oh, very well," he says, just as every subsequent husband has said under similar conditions a thousand times. "Oh, very well, have your own way. But I'm willing to risk a couple of the best city lots in this restricted residential district I can put my hand on the party who's been handing you that Santa Claus yarn, and not have to travel more than a quarter of a mile to do it either. I saw him talking with you yesterday while I was trying to teach the two Potomac shad how to swim. Eve, thank goodness I'm not jealous, and far be it from me to interfere with your friendships round the neighborhood—I guess things do get pretty lonely for you, hanging about the place all day—but if I were you I wouldn't waste much time in the company of that Snake. He's the worst he-gossip in Eden County. He'd make trouble for anybody in a holy minute if he got the chance."

Husbandlike, though, he follows her example and hangs up his fig leaf alongside of hers, upon the face of a nearby rock where a cleft in the cliff suggests a fireplace. Two minutes later he is snoring to beat the walrus, asleep in the next glade. But does the lady drop right off too? She lies down all right, after looking under the edge of the mossy bank for burglars, but she doesn't stay there.

As soon as everything is nice and quiet, up she gets. Stealthily she plucks an apple from that forbidden tree and stealthily she slips it down inside of Adam's fig leaf. After that she can hardly wait through the night for daylight to appear. When the first pink rays of the sunlight come stealing athwart the sward she is sitting up and poking Adam in the ribs.

"Oh, dearie," she cries in well-simulated surprise, "see what Santa has brought us—a lovely red apple."

And Adam falls for the deception. It is the original fall of man. Personally he doesn't care much for apples. Offhand he can think of a dozen things he likes better for breakfast. But, manlike, he humors her. He takes one bite, and then she snatches the apple away from him and eats all of it—slowly and distinctly.

You see it now, don't you—the true inwardness of the Christmas gift-giving habit as between married couples? She has gone through the form of giving him for Christmas the very thing that she wanted all along.

115

The Twelve Days of Christmas

On the first day of Christmas my true love sent to me
A partridge in a pear tree.

On the second day of Christmas my true love sent to me
Two turtle doves and a partridge in a pear tree.

On the third day of Christmas my true love sent to me
Three French hens,
Two turtle doves and a partridge in a pear tree.

On the fourth day of Christmas my true love sent to me
Four cawing birds, three French hens
Two turtle doves and a partridge in a pear tree.

On the fifth day of Christmas my true love sent to me
Five gold rings!
Four cawing birds, three French hens,
Two turtle doves and a partridge in a pear tree.

On the sixth day of Christmas my true love sent to me
Six geese a-laying,
Five gold rings!
Four cawing birds, three French hens,
Two turtle doves and a partridge in a pear tree.

On the seventh day of Christmas my true love sent to me
Seven swans a-swimming, six geese a-laying,
Five gold rings!
Four cawing birds, three French hens,
Two turtle doves and a partridge in a pear tree.

On the eighth day of Christmas my true love sent to me
Eight maids a-milking,
Seven swans a-swimming, six geese a-laying,
Five gold rings!

Four cawing birds, three French hens,
Two turtle doves and a partridge in a pear tree.

On the ninth day of Christmas my true love sent to me
Nine ladies dancing, eight maids a-milking,
Seven swans a-swimming, six geese a-laying,
Five gold rings!
Four cawing birds, three French hens,
Two turtle doves and a partridge in a pear tree.

On the tenth day of Christmas my true love sent to me
Ten lords a-leaping,
Nine ladies dancing, eight maids a-milking,
Seven swans a-swimming, six geese a-laying,
Five gold rings!
Four cawing birds, three French hens,
Two turtle doves and a partridge in a pear tree.

On the eleventh day of Christmas my true love sent to me
Eleven pipers piping, ten lords a-leaping,
Nine ladies dancing, eight maids a-milking,
Seven swans a-swimming, six geese a-laying,
Five gold rings!
Four cawing birds, three French hens,
Two turtle doves and a partridge in a pear tree.

On the twelfth day of Christmas my true love sent to me
Twelve drummers drumming,
Eleven pipers piping, ten lords a-leaping,
Nine ladies dancing, eight maids a-milking,
Seven swans a-swimming, six geese a-laying,
Five gold rings!
Four cawing birds, three French hens,
Two turtle doves,
And a partridge in a pear tree!

CELEBRATION

The Feast of Christmas

No one has in recent times written more lovingly of the glories of good eating than advertising executive Silas Spitzer. Writer and gourmet cook by avocation, he served as food editor for The Saturday Evening Post's *sister publication*, Holiday. *The following* selections are excerpted from articles he wrote for Christmas issues of Holiday *in the 1950's. The recipes are from New England food expert Charlotte Turgeon's collection of traditional American foods, reprinted from* The Saturday Evening Post All-American Cookbook.

The Christmas dinner of my youth was the longest, most lavish repast of the year. It took several days to prepare, needed extra help in the kitchen, and was so elaborate that it always strained the family's finances. It began with a crunching of salted nuts and a munching of celery at about two o'clock, and drifted, without coming to any definite conclusion, into a sort of contented stupor as the late afternoon shaded into twilight.

Even on ordinary occasions we were a tribe noted for our uninhibited appetites. But on Christmas, our number supplemented by relatives and close friends, we sat down to a table so heavily laden that it can only be described as medieval. If turkey or goose were the major element of this unbuttoned orgy, it was always a bird of monumental proportions, the largest the local market could supply. If roast beef held the place of honor, it was seven ribs thick, and loomed in its platter like Gibraltar.

Gravy was served in depth, homemade bread in huge, sweet-smelling loaves. Quantities of vegetables and minor accompaniments were handed around in overflowing bowls and tureens. In the largest of these vessels was a snowy pile of whipped potatoes, with rivulets of yellow butter running down its sides from a large chunk melting in a cavity at its peak. Another fixture was our mother's wonderful red cabbage, spicy with caraway seeds, rich with goose or chicken fat and piquant with the tart-sweet taste of green apples and sugar.

From year to year, there were few surprises in this most traditional of holiday menus, except on those last few occasions when the family still assembled in force. At these later gatherings, I seem to recall several new dishes of a spectacular modern sort, introduced by the eldest sister, who had suddenly become aware of the fascinations of fashionable living as reported in the glossy periodicals of that day. With her own fair hands, she prepared and served orange-flavored sweet potatoes buried under a froth of toasted marshmallow, odd-tasting artichokes with a thick yellow sauce that was slightly curdled, and a complicated dessert involving ladyfingers, jelly, whipped cream and candied violets.

These innovations, however, were consumed with curiosity rather than gusto, and were tolerated mainly to keep the family peace. For the greater part, our Christmas dinner progressed happily through the old familiar edibles and was crowned not only by mince pie and apple pie but by a sleek jet-black plum pudding that looked like an old-fashioned anarchist's bomb, and was just about as heavy. During the final languid hour, while the grownups smoked cigars and sipped muscatel or brandy, the younger element snapped frilly favors which blossomed into frivolous paper hats.

Many Americans no longer eat on such a formidable scale, but in spite of the present generation's daintier appetites, our native Christmas food and customs still largely follow the traditions established by our English forebears. In England's earlier times there were feasting and pageantry so magnificent that even Hollywood, in its gaudiest moments, has never quite succeeded in capturing their grandeur. For hundreds of years the great moment of these banquets was the joyous entrance of the cavalcade which brought in the boar's head garlanded with rosemary and bay, a lemon or a rosy apple clenched between its bristling tusks. It was carried aloft on a great platter to the sound of harps and the singing of carols. I had always conceived of the boar's head as having only symbolical significance, but I learned from recent reading that it was also a dish relished for its own sake. In its preparation, the head itself was boned and the inside coated with minced pig's liver, chopped apples, onion, sage and rosemary. It was then solidly stuff-

Strong, fast, ferocious, the boar was favorite quarry of Norman kings, who punished unprivileged killing of the beast by death.

119

ed with sausage meat, ox tongue, truffles, mushrooms, pistachio nuts and spices, moistened liberally with apple brandy and then boiled in a cloth for the better part of a day.

A hundred four roasted peacocks were served at one famous feudal feast, borne in single file by a procession of a hundred four servants, with an escort of candle bearers, minstrels and baying hounds. Each peacock had been stuffed with spices and wild herbs, its beak gilded, and its tail feathers replaced and fanned out to their full spread of opulent color. Less spectacular, but perhaps more satisfying in a gustatory sense, was a celebrated pie that once graced the banquet of an English nobleman. Under its mountainous crust it was laden with geese, rabbits, wild ducks, woodcocks, snipe, partridges, curlews, pigeons and blackbirds, and was brought to the guests on a cart that was specially built to carry it.

A poet of Elizabeth's time, boasting of country Christmases, writes of "their thirty-pound butter'd eggs, their pies of carps' tongues, their pheasants drenched with ambergris, the carcasses of three fat wethers bruised for gravy, to make sauce for a single peacock." As may be imagined, it took floods of drink to wash down these unctuous and heavily flavored courses—a circumstance that did nothing to hamper the boisterousness of the occasion.

Peacock, curlew, partridge, blackbird . . . These exotic birds may have been spectacular but they were surely less tender and flavorsome than the modern American turkey that is specially bred and carefully nurtured to grace the holiday table.

AMERICAN ROAST TURKEY WITH OYSTER STUFFING

12- to 14-pound turkey

Stuffing:
1 cup chopped celery
1 cup chopped onion
8 tablespoons butter
8 cups day-old soft bread crumbs

½ teaspoon powdered sage
½ teaspoon powdered thyme
½ teaspoon nutmeg
3 tablespoons chopped parsley
2 teaspoons salt
¼ teaspoon pepper
2 eggs, slightly beaten
1 pint oysters
1 teaspoon lemon juice

Gravy:
¾ cup fat
¾ cup flour
6 cups liquid
Parsley

If possible, buy a fresh turkey. If you are using the frozen variety thaw it completely before stuffing. Wipe the bird inside and out with a damp towel. Cut the neck off as close to the body as possible without cutting the skin. Cut off the wing tips. Rub a little salt and pepper into both the neck and body cavities. Keep the turkey in a cool place while preparing the stuffing.

Stuffing: Cook the chopped celery and onion in butter just until tender. Combine all the ingredients for the stuffing in a large bowl and toss well with a salad fork and spoon until thoroughly blended. The oysters should be left whole if very small, otherwise cut them in large pieces. Add any oyster liquor to the stuffing. Cool the stuffing before packing it loosely into the turkey cavities. Close both openings by sewing them up with kitchen thread or inserting small skewers and lacing the openings.

The Giblets: Place the wing tips, neck, heart and gizzard in 3 cups of water. Add ½ teaspoon salt, a small onion, a stalk of celery with leaves cut up, 1 small bay leaf and a small pinch of powdered thyme. Cover and simmer for 2 hours or cook in a pressure cooker for 15 to 20 minutes at 10-pound pressure. Set aside for use in making gravy.

Druids believed mistletoe sacred. Pliny thought it cured tumors and ulcers; at Christmas it has a happier usage.

To Truss: Cut 4 feet of kitchen twine and double it. Tie the midway point to the tail end of the turkey. Wind the twine around each wing and crisscross it across the body, drawing the wings to the sides of the bird. Bring the two pieces of twine forward to the leg tips and encircle each tip twice with the twine and draw the pieces together to bind the legs to the body. Cross the twine once more over the body, turn the bird over and tie. Remove string before serving.

Roasting: Place the turkey breast side up on a rack in a large roasting pan. Rub the entire surface with melted butter or margarine. Place the turkey in a 300-degree oven and allow 25 minutes per pound for a bird of 12 pounds or less; 18 minutes per pound is sufficient for a larger bird. Baste the bird every 15 minutes for the first hour and every 30 minutes thereafter: *or,* after the first hour, cover the bird with aluminum foil or with a large piece of cheesecloth thoroughly saturated in melted butter and discontinue the basting process. There is nothing really as good as continued basting, however. Sprinkle with salt and pepper 1 hour before the end of cooking time and roast the liver for the last 45 minutes only.

Gravy: Place the turkey and liver on a large platter. Pour off all the fat from the roasting pan. Measure and put back ¾ cup of the fat. Heat until it bubbles. Add the flour and stir hard, scraping the juices from the bottom of the pan. When well blended and browned, add 6 cups of liquid including the strained giblet broth. Stir until smooth and thickened. Strain into two heated gravy bowls, adding the chopped giblets to one only, since some like them and some, particularly children, don't.

To Serve: Surround the turkey with a garland of parsley and serve with pride.

GERMAN RED CABBAGE

6 tablespoons fat (chicken*, goose, duck or bacon)
1 large onion, chopped
2 tablespoons sugar
6 cups shredded red cabbage
4 cooking apples, peeled, cored and sliced
3 tablespoons cider vinegar
2 teaspoons salt
½ teaspoon black pepper
Bouillon or water

Heat the liquid fat in a deep pan. Add the onions and the sugar and cook until the onion is soft and the sugar slightly caramelized. Add the rest of the ingredients except for the bouillon and stir well. Add just enough bouillon or water to come to the surface of the cabbage. Cover and cook very slowly or in a 275-degree oven for 3 hours. For highest flavor let the cabbage stand in a cool place overnight and reheat in a serving casserole.

*Chicken, goose or duck fat can be melted (tried out) in the top of a double boiler over simmering water.

The Festive Christmas Goose

There is no more tantalizing aroma in all cookery than the smell of a fine goose, browning slowly in the oven. Along about noon of Christmas Day, as in centuries past, this magic fragrance will drift from the kitchens of fortunate homes in many lands. As the dinner hour approaches, it will penetrate to the far corners of the household, bringing to those within its spell a vision of meltingly tender dark meat under a skin of crackling crispness, of mounds of savory stuffing, and of rivers of rich and steaming gravy.

Roast goose has crowned the Christmas feast of tradition since the Middle Ages. In Charlemagne's time, landowners were taxed a specified quantity of fattened geese, to be delivered to the imperial household on demand. Fat Henry VIII of England, using both fists, often consumed an entire roast goose at a sitting. Festooned with elaborate garlands, it was a Yuletide offering at the court of Louis XIV, whose custom it was to sit in lonely grandeur at a table elevated above the rest of the diners, his assembled guests.

Over the years more than any other people, the English have been deeply loyal to the Christmas goose. "For the goose is

Stomachs battle with manners but we manage to contain ourselves.

man's comfort in peace, sleepinge and wakinge," wrote Roger Ascham, tutor to the first Queen Elizabeth. When Dickens set out to describe the joyful excitement of Christmas dinner at the Cratchits, his inevitable choice for the climax of that great occasion was the entry of The Goose. The passage is a happy family classic. "There never was such a goose," it begins. "Bob said he didn't believe there ever was such a goose cooked."

And, if you recall, that amazing bird, big as it was, was consumed, to Mrs. Cratchit's delight, down to—"one small atom of a bone."

Except for minor variations and personal whims, goose is roasted according to the same general scheme in all countries. But, while roasting may follow a universally basic plan, there are almost as many ways of stuffing the Christmas bird as there are cooks.

In France, good red wine and garlic are rubbed into the skin and insides, and a simple dressing is made of the liver, bread and herbs.

Many German and Scandinavian cooks contrast the opulent sweetness of the meat with a tart stuffing of apples, cranberries and raisins. Danish goose is often crammed with dried apples and prunes, which swell during the cooking, absorbing just enough of the fat to make a fabulous eating with a crisp drumstick or a slice of sherry-basted breast.

A favorite Yugoslavian recipe calls for stuffing with wine-soaked sauerkraut. Wash a pound of sauerkraut in hot water, and squeeze dry. Melt a tablespoon of butter in a saucepan and sauté a chopped shallot and a few sliced scallions. Add an apple, peeled and diced, a bay leaf, 1 teaspoon of sugar, a little chopped parsley, a few caraway seeds, and the drained sauerkraut with an optional glassful of dry white wine. After simmering 30 minutes, the stuffing may be placed in the cavity of the bird.

The Irish, who are passionately fond of goose, are still loyal to a substantial padding of mashed potatoes and onions.

In our own country, the traditional turkey dressing of sage-flavored bread is still used by most cooks. But recently there has been a discernible trend to more imaginative ingredients, such as wild rice, celery and olives, peanuts, Brazil nuts, prunes, apples, cornbread, mushrooms and oysters.

There are those who think that roast goose needs no fancy trimmings and hold that only two side dishes are worthy of its presence. One is homemade applesauce, flavored with lemon and cinnamon or nutmeg. The other is a mountain of snowy whipped potatoes, smoking hot in a tureen, yearning for its benediction of ruddy gravy. Many North European families never serve roast goose without red cabbage, cooked with butter, wine or vine-

123

gar, sliced apple and caraway seeds. For drink upon this great occasion, the French ransack the cellar for the oldest and noblest bottle of red Burgundy or Bordeaux. The Germans quaff an amber Wurzburger, or some other mellow beer with a creamy head. Scandinavians first condition their innards with a few quick swallows of *aquavit*. In our own native land, we may drink any beverage from iced tea to sweet cider, but if we are wise we will prefer a fine California Cabernet, or Pinot Rouge.

To achieve a splendor worthy of the day, Christmas dinner should mount from climax to climax. Each course should depart from the commonplace, be flavored with surprise and garnished with love. The appearance of the goose, plump with its burden of hidden riches, will provide a peak of excitement. This is the moment which Zola depicted so glowingly amidst the gloomy pages of *L'Assommoir*: "When the goose was on the table, huge and golden, and running with gravy, it was not begun all at once. A sort of respectful wonderment silenced every tongue. What a devilish fine fat bird it was. What legs! What breast!"

The host's carving knife and steel flash above the stately fowl. With a touch of the blade, the drumsticks melt from their mooring. Quick strokes along the side of the breastbone release slices of succulent meat. A long-handled silver spoon is plunged deep, and a gush of steaming hot dressing bursts forth, dispersing a perfume of onions, sausage and herbs. Plates are filled with generous helpings, piled high with vegetables, drenched with gravy. The taste of the goose is even better than the aroma of its cooking. And now the family will understand why roast goose is not eaten every day, or even every month, but reserved for the one great day when all things must be wonderful.

ROAST GOOSE

12- to 14-pound goose

Stuffing:
5 cups soft bread crumbs
8 tablespoons butter, melted

½ cup grated onion
1 cup celery with leaves, chopped
1 cup diced tart peeled apple
1 teaspoon salt
½ teaspoon sage
¼ teaspoon nutmeg
¼ teaspoon thyme
¼ teaspoon black pepper
1 cup dry white wine

Wipe the bird inside and out, removing any yellow globules of fat. Place the fat in the top of a double boiler and let it cook over boiling water until all the liquid has been extracted. To save fuel, cook the giblets with ½ onion, a few celery leaves, a small bay leaf and a sprig of thyme in the bottom of the double boiler. Both operations take 1½ to 2 hours.

To Stuff: Break day-old bread into small crumbs in a bowl. Add the remaining ingredients and toss well. Chill in the refrigerator. Rub the inside of the bird with a little salt and put in the stuffing. Put most of the stuffing in the body cavity and the rest in the neck cavity. Sew the edges of the body opening together or use small skewers and lace them together. Tie the legs and wings together. Fold the neck skin over the opening and fasten it with a small skewer. Tie the legs and wings to the body with kitchen twine. Tie the leg ends together. If the goose is not to be roasted until some time later, keep it wrapped in the refrigerator.

To Roast: Preheat the oven to 325 degrees F. Prick the bird around the legs and wings with a fork and place it on a rack in an open roasting pan. Rub the skin with salt and pepper. Allow 25 minutes to the pound. Remove the fat from the pan every 30 minutes with a bulb baster. Save it for future use.

The Gravy: Place the roasted goose on a heated platter and pour off all the fat from the pan except for ¼ cup. Sprinkle with 4 tablespoons of flour and stir well, scraping all the juices adhering to the pan with a fork. As soon

From every mountainside, people, never empty-handed, come home for the holidays.

as the flour is well mixed stir in the strained giblet broth and enough water or chicken broth to measure 2 cups. Stir until thick and smooth. Strain the gravy into a small saucepan. Add the giblets, chopped rather fine, reheat the gravy and serve in a small bowl or gravy boat.

The Liver: While the gravy is being prepared, broil or pan-broil the liver 2 to 3 minutes on each side. Spread with butter and sprinkle with salt, pepper and lemon juice. Cut into 4 pieces and serve only to those who appreciate it.

SPICY APPLESAUCE

5 pounds cooking apples
2 cups water
1½ cups sugar
¼ teaspoon salt
½ teaspoon cinnamon
¼ teaspoon cloves
¼ teaspoon nutmeg
1 teaspoon vanilla

Core, peel and slice the apples. Put them in a heavy kettle with the water, sugar and spices. Cover and simmer until the apples are tender. Put them through a food mill. If the sauce is too liquid, boil it down over a moderate flame, stirring constantly, until thick. Add the vanilla.

APPLEJACK MINCEMEAT

2 pounds lean venison or beef, chopped or ground
1 pound suet, chopped or ground
6 cups cubed apples
1 pound currants
1 pound seedless raisins
1 pound muscat raisins
1 pound store-bought diced candied
  fruit (orange, citron, cherries, lemon)
3 cups brown sugar
2 teaspoons salt
1 teaspoon cinnamon
½ teaspoon cloves
1 teaspoon allspice
1 teaspoon nutmeg
2 to 3 cups water
2 cups applejack

Combine all the ingredients except for the applejack in a heavy kettle or casserole. Stir well and add enough water to make the mixture quite moist. Cover and barely simmer for 2 to 3 hours. Stir occasionally, adding more water if necessary.

When cooked, the mincemeat should be fairly dry. Stir in the applejack and pack into pint jars or cool and pack into containers for freezing. This recipe makes 10 pints, enough for 5 large pies.

Christmas Plum Pudding

In the opinion of all Englishmen and most Americans, this noblest specimen of the race of puddings is the only dessert blessed with the authentic look and flavor of Christmas. When it is brought in with fitting ceremony on a silver tray, its swelling façade decked with holly and enveloped in a blue nimbus of blazing brandy, it never fails to awaken a chorus of joyful praise, whether the diners resemble Dickens' humble Cratchits or look more like characters plucked all aglitter from the pages of the newest social register, *Who's Who*, or *Burke's Peerage*.

The earliest recorded version of plum pudding was much eaten, appropriately enough, during the reign of Queen Anne, that indulgent, overstuffed monarch who suffered from the gout. It was a sort of porridge made by thickening mutton broth with brown bread, contained raisins and spices, and was served in great smoking tureens as a first course at feasts. From this rude beginning evolved the plum pudding as we know it today—

The journey from kitchen to table is fraught with perils—loose carpet, errant toys, eager family pets.

127

firm and solid, sleekly rounded, dark and gleaming of complexion, and filled to bursting with every sort of fruit and sweetmeat except—and this is rather odd—plums.

In the family recipe favored by the British Royal Household, there are more than twenty separate ingredients, each sanctified by generations of use. To create a dish of such magnificence is not a simple or casual undertaking, especially when it involves the resources of the average modest home. According to classic admonition handed down from early Victorian times, a proper Christmas pudding takes "three days to cook, three weeks to set and ripen." Its preparation usually calls for the loving cooperation of all family, not excepting small boys and girls, with or without the assistance of their pets.

Many Americans of an older generation will recall with sentimental fondness the childish parts they once played in their own domestic version of this preholiday orgy of wonderful sights, sounds and smells. They needed little urging to rally round, to run swift errands, or to help in the actual kitchen tasks. There was work enough for everybody during those jolly, bustling days. Small boys cracked and picked nuts and, if they could be trusted to wield a knife, were put to slicing and shredding chunks of translucent, sugar-crusted citron and the ruddy peels of candied fruit. Fat, gleaming raisins and golden currants were washed and picked, then segregated in neat piles for weighing and mixing. A faint but persistent fragrance lingers in the memory of cinnamon and mace, of ginger and cloves, not to mention the exciting bouquet of brandy and rum which had been boldly filched from Papa's treasured supply.

Many families clung to an old custom which proclaimed that everybody, from the head of the house to the smallest high-chair tenant, took turns at stirring the pudding, "for luck." The culminating act took place when the dark, suety mixture was tied tightly in a floured cloth or pressed into a bowl and lowered into a kettle of furiously boiling water for at least six hours.

Certain cynics maintain that plum pudding is a decorative symbol, not a delicacy for the gourmet, and that it is frequently eaten only because of the spirits which saturate it, or the hard sauce which bears it company. Any attempt, they add, to do it justice after a man has packed away several ample helpings of soup, roast turkey and the usual fixings, is a simple invitation to calamity. But less delicate and more capacious mortals sharply disagree, among them some of the great names of English literature.

Nobody has ever written of food or feasting as well as Charles Dickens, and the classic description in *A Christmas Carol* of the anxiously awaited pudding that blessed the Cratchits' Yuletide dinner forever captures the excitement and glory of that wonderful occasion:

"In half a minute Mrs. Cratchit entered—flushed, but smiling proudly—with the pudding, like a speckled cannonball, so hard and firm blazing in half of half-a-quartern of ignited brandy, and bedight with Christmas holly stuck into the top."

Indeed, the costliness of this opulent dessert and the time consumed in its making are mitigated by the fact that, like all things of character and worth, it actually improves with age. As most good cooks know, it should be wrapped carefully, put away in the pantry and given occasional refreshing draughts of brandy or rum to keep its spirits up. Then, six months after its holiday debut, it may be served in thinly sliced helpings on some special occasion, thus providing a delightful premonition of Christmas at a time when roses and strawberries fill the garden.

HOLIDAY PLUM PUDDING

Makes 10 to 12 servings.
1 cup finely chopped beef suet (¼ pound)
1 cup plus 2 tablespoons brown sugar
½ cup milk
2 eggs, well beaten
1 cup currants
1 pound chopped mixed fruits (cherries, citron, orange peel, lemon peel)
1 cup sliced blanched almonds
1¼ cups sifted all-purpose flour

Extravagantly fueled on brandy or rum, with calories and conscience disregarded, the great pudding is the crown of the feast day.

1 teaspoon baking soda
1 teaspoon salt
½ teaspoon nutmeg
1 teaspoon cinnamon
¼ teaspoon mace
1 cup soft bread crumbs
½ cup brandy

Combine suet, brown sugar, milk and eggs. Mix fruits and almonds with ¼ cup of the flour. Sift remaining flour with soda, salt and spices. Add fruits, crumbs and flour-and-spice mixture to suet mixture. Mix well. Turn into well-greased 1-quart covered pudding mold. Steam 3 hours. (*Steaming directions*: Use steamer or deep covered kettle. In using kettle, place filled and covered mold on trivet or wire rack in kettle. Pour in boiling water to ½ depth of mold. Place cover on kettle and steam, replenishing the boiling water when necessary to keep the proper level of ½ depth of mold.) Turn out on hot platter, heat brandy in small saucepan, pour over pudding, light brandy and bring pudding to the table flaming. Serve with hard sauce.

HARD SAUCE

½ cup butter; dash of salt
2 cups sifted confectioners' sugar
Brandy if desired

Soften butter; beat in sugar until light and fluffy. Add brandy to taste, beating it in thoroughly. To serve, spoon over thin slices of pudding.

Sweetmeats and Sugarplums

FRUITCAKE BARS

1 can (6 ounces) frozen concentrated orange juice,
  thawed, undiluted
½ cup and 2/3 cup packed light brown sugar,
  divided
1 cup raisins
1 package (8 ounces) pitted dates, chopped
1 jar (1 pound) mixed candied fruit, finely chopped
½ cup soft butter or margarine
4 eggs
1 cup unsifted all-purpose flour
1/8 teaspoon baking soda
½ teaspoon cinnamon
½ teaspoon nutmeg
¼ teaspoon allspice
¼ teaspoon cloves
1 cup chopped nuts

In medium saucepan combine undiluted concentrated orange juice and ½ cup brown sugar. Stir over low heat until mixture comes to a boil. Add raisins and dates, bring to a boil again. Remove from heat, stir in mixed candied fruit and set aside.

In large bowl cream butter and remaining 2/3 cup brown sugar. Beat in eggs, one at a time. Blend in flour, baking soda, cinnamon, nutmeg, allspice and cloves. Stir in nuts and fruit mixture. Turn into 2 waxed paper-lined 15-by-10-by-1-inch baking pans. Bake in 300-degree oven 35 to 40 minutes, or until cake tester inserted in center comes out clean.

When cool, frost with orange glaze (see recipe below). Cut into 3-by-1-inch bars. Garnish with halved candied cherries. Makes about 100 bars.

ORANGE GLAZE

1½ cups sifted confectioners' sugar
¼ cup orange juice
1 tablespoon soft butter or margarine

In small bowl mix all ingredients until smooth.

WALNUT KISSES

3 egg whites
1/8 teaspoon salt
2 cups sifted confectioners' sugar
¾ teaspoon vanilla
¼ teaspoon almond extract
2 teaspoons water
1 cup chopped walnuts

Preheat the oven to 225 degrees F. Use Teflon-coated baking sheets or line metal baking sheets with brown paper.

Beat the egg whites and salt until stiff but still moist. Add the sugar slowly and alternately with a mixture of the extracts and water which is added drop by drop. When very thick and glossy fold in the nutmeats.

Drop by half-teaspoonfuls onto the baking sheet. Bake 40 to 45 minutes. Remove from the pan while hot. Makes 40 to 50 small cookies.

GINGERBREAD BOYS AND GIRLS

½ cup butter
½ cup margarine
1½ cups sugar
1 egg
2 tablespoons dark corn syrup
4 teaspoons grated orange rind
3 cups all-purpose unbleached flour
2 teaspoons soda
2 teaspoons cinnamon
1 teaspoon ginger
½ teaspoon nutmeg
½ teaspoon cloves
½ teaspoon salt

Blend the butter and margarine and gradually beat in the sugar until light and fluffy. Add the egg and beat until smooth.

Add the corn syrup and orange peel and mix.

Sift all the dry ingredients and stir into the butter

mixture. Form the dough into a ball and wrap it in wax paper. Chill in the refrigerator.

Preheat the oven to 375 degrees F. Roll out the dough on a lightly floured surface to a thickness of ¼ inch. Cut with a gingerbread-boy cutter. To differentiate between the sexes, cut out small triangular pieces and put on the sides of some of the heads to look like hair ribbons.

Place on ungreased baking sheets 1 inch apart. Bake 8 to 10 minutes. Allow to stand 2 minutes on the pans before transferring to a wire rack to cool. Makes 18 to 24, depending on size.

CANDIED ORANGE SLICES

6 oranges
Water
1½ cups packed dark brown sugar
2 cups water
Granulated sugar

Place oranges in large saucepan or kettle. Cover with water. Cover and bring to a boil over medium heat. Reduce heat and simmer 40 minutes, or until peel is tender. Drain and cool.

Cut oranges into 3/8-inch crosswise slices and cut slices in half; place in bowl. In medium saucepan mix together brown sugar and water. Stir over low heat until sugar dissolves and mixture comes to a boil. Boil, stirring frequently, for 20 minutes or until thick and syrupy. Pour over orange slices. Cover and refrigerate overnight.

Remove orange slices from syrup and roll in granulated sugar; place on rack to dry overnight. Roll in sugar again just before packing in gift boxes. Makes 6 cups.

POPCORN BALLS

2/3 cup granulated sugar
½ cup water
3 tablespoons white corn syrup
1/8 teaspoon salt
1 teaspoon vanilla
½ teaspoon vinegar

Prepare about 6 cups of popped corn, allowing a little extra if there are helpers who will eat some while waiting for the syrup to cook.

To prepare syrup, combine sugar, water and corn syrup in a large aluminum saucepan. Stir until sugar is dissolved, then cook without stirring until the firm ball stage is reached (248 degrees F on a candy thermometer). Add salt, vanilla and vinegar and continue cooking until a little syrup dropped into cold water forms brittle threads (firm crack stage, or 290 degrees F). Pour syrup over popped corn in a large mixing bowl.

As soon as it is cool enough to handle, spread butter on your hands and use them to mix thoroughly and shape into balls.

CANDIED APPLES

10 to 12 medium red apples
10 to 12 wooden sticks (skewers)
2 cups sugar
1 cup light corn syrup
½ cup water
2 teaspoons cinnamon
Red food coloring (about ½ teaspoon)

Wash and dry apples. Insert stick in stem end of each.

Combine other ingredients. Heat slowly, stirring constantly until sugar dissolves. Bring to a boil and boil rapidly to the soft-crack stage (280 degrees on a candy thermometer).

Remove from heat. As soon as bubbling stops, begin dipping apples. Tilt pan and swirl apples through, letting surplus syrup drip off. Place on greased cookie sheet to cool, spaced well apart so apples will not touch.

If syrup becomes too thick, reheat slightly over low heat. For last few apples, stand apple in saucepan and spoon remaining syrup up and over it.

Three to five minutes after dipping, shift apples on the cookie sheet to prevent sticking. When cool, wrap individually in waxed paper or plastic.

Tied with bright yarn or ribbon, the popcorn balls can serve as tree ornaments.

O Little Town of Bethlehem

Phillips Brooks

Lewis H. Redner

Christmas · sing merrilie

The deeply philosophical words of "O Little Town of Bethlehem" were written by a Boston minister and theologian, Phillips Brooks.

God Rest Ye Merry, Gentlemen

1. God rest ye mer - ry, gen - tle-men, Let noth-ing you dis - may, For
2. From God, our Heav-en - ly Fa - ther, A bless-ed an - gel came, And
3. The shep-herds at these ti - dings Re - joic-ed much in mind, And

Je - sus Christ, our Sa - vi - our, Was born up - on this day: To
un - to cer - tain shep-herds Brought ti - dings of the same: How
left their flocks a - feed - ing In tem-pest, storm and wind, And

save us all from Sa - tan's pow'r, When we were gone a - stray:
that in Beth - le - hem was born The Son of God by name:
went to Beth - le - hem straight way, The Bless-ed Babe to find:
O ——

ti - dings of com-fort and joy, Com-fort and joy, O ti - dings of com-fort and joy.

Traditional English Melody

Traditional English Words

God rest ye merrie Gentlemen

The form of this London melody, popular in English towns in the eighteenth century, was influenced by street ballads and round singing.

Silent Night

1. Si - lent night, Ho - ly night, All is calm, all is bright.
2. Si - lent night, Ho - ly night, Shep - herds quake at the sight.
3. Si - lent night, Ho - ly night, Son of God, love's pure light.

'Round yon Vir - gin Moth - er and Child Ho - ly In - fant so ten - der and mild,
Glo - ries stream from heav - en a - far, Heav'n - ly hosts sing Al - le - lu - ia;
Ra - diant beams from Thy ho - ly face, With the dawn of re - deem - ing grace,

Sleep in heav - en - ly peace,___ Sleep in heav - en - ly peace.___
Christ the Sa - vior is born,___ Christ the Sa - vior is born.___
Je - sus, Lord, at Thy birth,___ Je - sus, Lord, at Thy birth.___

Joseph Mohr

Franz Gruber

The music of the world's best loved Christmas carol was written by Franz Gruber, an Austrian church organist, in 1818.

O Come, All Ye Faithful

English translation, Rev. Frederick Oakeley

Latin Hymn, Attributed to John Reading

"Adeste Fideles" is a Latin hymn to be sung with dignity and voices in unison. The tempo lends itself well to processions.

Things To Do

Maybe getting ready for Christmas is the very best part of the holiday season.

Children know. Long after they have forgotten gifts received they may remember red-and-green paper chains carried home from kindergarten, the desk blotter laboriously assembled for father at Cub Scout meetings, the lopsided pincushion made for mother.

What is the magic of the handmade gift or decoration?

It comes from the heart—witness the bloodstains from pricked finger and hammered thumb.

It's one of a kind. Individually planned for a special person or a special place in the home. Assembled with happy anticipation and loving thoughts as well as tape and glue.

The projects suggested on these pages are not ones you can begin the day before Christmas. You will need to start these early—and you should have children to help you, because children are far better at finding acorns and bird's nests, seed pods and pine cones, than grown-ups are.

Decorate a Pioneer-Style Tree

When the main house at Conner Prairie Pioneer Settlement was built in 1823 it was the only brick residence in Central Indiana and the finest homestead for miles around. Today the spacious two-story home near Noblesville is the centerpiece of a "living museum" complex where visitors see costumed men and women working at tasks that were commonplace in pioneer days but are almost forgotten today.

Conner Prairie is closed in winter except for two weekends just before Christmas, when it is lit by candles and decorated as it might have been for a holiday season in the 1830's. There's a punchbowl, fruit and fancy cookies in the dining room; bread and pies are being made in the kitchen. The brightest quilts and embroidered coverlets are displayed on four-posters in bedrooms that are fragrant with pomander balls and tiny nosegays of dried flowers. Tradition has it these were gifts for holiday guests to take home with them.

In the spacious living room, where tiny-paned windows with ruffled curtains overlook the White River, stands a Christmas tree thought to be like the very first ones seen in the Midwest.

The tree itself is a red cedar, slender and prickly and quite different from the horizontal-branching firs and spruces we use for Christmas trees today. The red cedar is the only evergreen native to central Indiana, so it would have been the only kind available to the pioneers.

The ornaments hung on the tree are all ones mentioned in old letters or diaries of the place and period—red apples, cookies, tiny cornhusk dolls, and Bible verses printed on scraps of parchment and hung from the tree's twigs with bits of bright yarn. There are strings of popcorn but no cranberries, as cranberries don't grow wild in Indiana and the pioneers wouldn't have had them. Instead there are red and orange rose-hips. Bits of sheep's-wool are laid on the branches, to look like snow.

Recently a research historian reported finding a mention of another kind of tree ornament—a tiny basket made of half an eggshell with a bit of ribbon glued to it for a handle, filled with nutmeats and small bits of candy. Might such baskets have hung on the tree as gifts for visiting children, as the spice balls and nosegays were gifts for the ladies who came to call? No one is sure, but the ladies who serve as guides and hostesses at Conner Prairie are saving washed and dried eggshell halves which they will hang on next year's pioneer Christmas tree.

THINGS TO HANG ON YOUR TREE

The tree decorated at home for family and friends need not follow the rules of historical authenticity so closely as the Conner Prairie tree, which is displayed in a museum setting and sponsored by an educational institution.

Volunteer hostesses and their young helpers dress the part of pioneers to ready Conner Prairie for Christmas visitors. On the prickly cedar tree go cookies and popcorn, gingerbread boys and girls (see recipe on page 130) and cornhusk dolls. Cornhusks are easy to work with if they are moistened with water to which a few drops of glycerine have been added, to keep them soft and pliable. One easy way to make a cornhusk doll is to start with a wooden clothespin. Fold the husks around it and tie with yarn or raffia at the doll's neck, waist, and wrists.

At home, you can use a nursery-grown spruce or any other kind of tree you like. You can string cranberries, even if they don't grow wild in your part of the country. You can design your own ornaments and make them from a variety of materials, so long as you keep to the spirit of pioneer days.

Apples, popcorn and cranberries: Apples are quite heavy, so choose the smaller sizes and provide a sturdy hanger. One way: run stiff wire down through the core and twist the end around a cinnamon stick to keep it from pulling out. Later you can eat the apples and use the cinnamon sticks to stir mugs of hot cider.

To make garlands, use the largest needles you have and the heavy thread marked "Button and Carpet." Try to buy a brand of popcorn that turns out large and fluffy, and aim the needle through the largest and most solid segment. Very often the popcorn breaks apart as the needle goes through (in that case, the stringer gets to eat the fragments.) Children may find it easier and more satisfying to string cranberries and merely *eat* popcorn. You can string popcorn and cranberries separately, or combine them.

After Christmas, hang the garlands outdoors for the birds to enjoy.

COOKIES—TO EAT OR TO LOOK AT:

If cookies are to hang on the tree as ornaments, they should have holes made in them before they are baked. You can run narrow ribbon or yarn through the hole (after the cookie cools) but an easier way is to hang the cookie from a clean pipe cleaner bent into S-shape. To make inedible cookies that can be saved from year to year, mix 2 cups of flour and 1 cup of salt with enough water to make a stiff dough. Roll, cut with fancy cutters, make hole for hanging, and bake 2 hours in a slow oven (250 degrees F). Decorate with paint or with glued-on seeds. Store wrapped in tissue paper, in a dry, airy place.

If you like needlework, cut traditional cookie shapes (bell, star, angel, reindeer) from felt, two at a time. No seam allowance is needed. Overcast along the edges with matching thread, stuffing a little cotton inside before sewing the last side. Trim with stitched-on or glued-on rickrack, ribbon and bits of contrasting felt.

Make a "Tree" of Weeds and Flowers

Lois Douglas starts thinking about Christmas in June. That's when she begins drying roses, daisies and other flowers that will reappear later in the Christmas decorations she makes. Her big harvest comes in September and October, when she drives out in the country to gather roadside weeds: teasel, goldenrod, ironweed. She gets bearded wheat and cornhusks from farmers; she brings moss and grapevines from the woods. Mrs. Douglas has even found a way to use hedge apples, the pimply, green, strong-smelling fruits regarded as a nuisance by everyone else who finds them along the roadside.

To dry and preserve these natural materials Mrs. Douglas uses a variety of techniques. Some flowers are dried in a microwave oven, others are buried in silica gel or sand. Some—like the big blossoms of hydrangea and snowball bush—are simply left where they grow, to dry on their own stems until harvest time. Weeds are generally tied in bunches and hung head down from the garage rafters. Leaves are placed like bouquets in vases of glycerine-and-water solution for several weeks, a method of preservation that leaves them leathery but supple. The hedge apples are sliced and then dried all day in a very slow oven—the result, cup-shaped and fluted, looks like a big poppy blossom.

"There are a lot of good books on drying flowers," Mrs. Douglas says. "If you're interested, read one or two, then start experimenting. You have to learn to use the plant materials available in your part of the country, and get the kind of effect you like. So try different methods, and see how things turn out."

Many natural materials have interesting textures or shapes but are dull brown or gray. Mrs. Douglas tints these, because she likes a variety of soft colors to work with. She has a special fondness for shades of pink, lavender and purples ("Purple is the color of the church season of Advent, leading up to the birth of Christ, so it's appropriate for the decorations you display during the weeks before Christmas."), but she also uses blue, yellow and gold.

"The dark green of pine branches can be a cold color; the bright red so often used with it can be harsh," Mrs. Douglas says. "Too, people get tired of red and green at Christmas. Why not pink, purple, gold, soft green? These are colors of life and joy, and surely life and joy *is* the message of Christmas."

TINTING DRIED PLANT MATERIALS

There are two methods for coloring dried plant materials; you can use either spray paint or liquid dye (RIT is the brand generally available).

When painting, Mrs. Douglas never uses just one can of spray paint. She buys a number of different shades of different colors. She spreads the dry weeds or leaves on a plastic dropcloth on the garage floor, then starts experimenting. A little of one color, then a little of another produces a softer, more interesting effect than one color alone.

Cornhusks and hydrangea blossoms can be successfully tinted by dipping them in liquid dye and then hanging them on the clothesline to drip-dry. Some dark materials can be successfully bleached in a Chlorox solution and then tinted a light or bright color with dye.

MAKING A DRIED PLANT "TREE"

The pastel-colored "tree" displayed on Mrs. Douglas's coffee table is made of tinted plant materials mounted on a yard-high cone of wire mesh. She also makes a five-foot "tree" for her home, and she has helped to make two fifteen-foot-tall ones for decorating the sanctuary of the North Methodist Church in Indianapolis.

To make the table-size one, buy 36-inch wire mesh from a hardware store. This comes with ¼- or ½-inch holes in it; she likes the ¼-inch kind best. Mark first, then cut with a tin-snips 4 triangular sections, each 15 inches wide at the base and 36 inches tall.

Shape each triangle by rolling it a little, then put them

142

Every year Lois Douglas helps to decorate her church with dried flowers and other plant materials. At right: A fifteen-foot-tall tree stands at the altar, with a life-size papier-mâché Madonna for visual accent. The small pictures show grapevine garlands and sunburst arrangements of tinted weeds that decorate side walls of the sanctuary. Below, left: Priscilla Douglas, following her mother's directions, completes a thirty-six-inch tree for her Chicago apartment.

together so as to form a cone. Overlap the cut edges and fasten them together with short bits of wire. The resulting frame need not be neat, as it will be entirely covered.

When the frame is ready, place it in the middle of a plastic dropcloth or old bedsheet and start applying your dried, tinted plant materials. Flowers with stems are easiest to attach—just tuck their stems into the holes in the wire mesh. Other materials—such as the dried hedge apple slices and cornhusk pompons—need to be wired in place.

The trick is to mix colors and textures tastefully as you cover the "tree" frame. Helpful hints: Use very fine-textured, lacy materials in bunches, so they don't disappear. Use large materials—like the cornhusk bows and hydrangea blossoms—singly and spaced well apart. The colors will harmonize if they are all soft rather than harsh colors.

"Use your imagination," she suggests. "There are no hard and fast rules to follow, and no two decorations will ever be alike."

Make Pomander Balls

These spicy balls can serve as decorations that scent the whole house for Christmas. They are also nice gifts that children can make for aunts and grandmothers who will find that a pomander ball hung in the closet will keep things sweet-smelling for a year or longer.

Start making pomander balls at least six weeks before Christmas to allow time for them to dry completely before they are used as decorations or gifts.

The pomander ball's sweet, spicy scent will linger like a memory of Christmas cheer.

You will need medium-sized oranges, a great many whole cloves, powdered orris root, ground cinnamon, and a steel knitting needle or something similar to pierce the orange rind. Begin by sticking cloves in the orange

until it is entirely covered. Children enjoy this task, which is sweet-smelling and not too demanding, as the cloves need not be set in rows or any pattern.

Mix together equal parts of orris root and cinnamon and roll the balls in this powder until they are well coated. (Use cinnamon alone if orris root is not available.) Then wrap loosely in tissue paper and leave in a warm, dry place. Inspect from time to time—if the balls are drying too fast they may shrivel, and if too slowly they may mildew. When dry, shake off the surplus powder and trim with ribbons.

Apples, pears, or lemons may be used to make pomander balls of slightly different shapes and sizes.

Make a Woodland Wreath

"My wreath is the product of many hours of work and many sore fingers," says Judy Horn of Dayton, Ohio. "There are no shortcuts. Each nut and pine cone must first be attached to a length of wire, then the wire must be securely fastened to the wreath frame. All this takes

time, but the result is a sturdy wreath that will last a lifetime, and one that looks so nice you'll want to leave it up year-round."

Only a few tools are needed: a good pair of pliers with wire-cutter, a drill (hand or electric) with a small bit, and some kind of vise or clamp to hold nuts while you drill holes through them.

Buy a wire wreath frame from a craft shop or florists' supply house (the wreath shown was constructed on an eighteen-inch frame). You will also need a spool of No. 24 wire, florists' tape, and clear acrylic spray.

Pine cones come in many different sizes and they fall from the trees at different seasons (some in early spring). They should be collected when they fall, as they turn dark and brittle if left on the ground. Try to collect a number of middle-sized cones of the same size and type, for edging the wreath.

Wash cones with the garden hose to remove dust and insects. Store in wooden crates or mesh bags, in a dry place where air can circulate through them.

Collect nuts, acorns and buckeyes in autumn. Spread them on old cookie tins and bake them (20 minutes at 300 degrees F) to kill any insects or larvae they might contain. Preserve some nuts in their hulls, and some extra pieces of hull, for variety. Other seeds and pods may be used, if they are sturdy and a good color—

About 100 pine cones and 100 nuts go into making the woodland wreath, shown completed and as construction is begun.

dried peach pits and the prickly seed pods from sweetgum trees are suitable. Crack some nuts in half and pick out the nutmeats, as the inside of the shell has an interesting pattern. If walnuts and hickory nuts can't be found in the woods where you live, substitute pecans or English walnuts from the supermarket.

Store these materials in mesh bags hung from the rafters, with a few mothballs in each bag to discourage insects or rodents, until you assemble the wreath.

Begin by wrapping all parts of the wire frame with

florists' tape. This helps to keep the wired-on cones from slipping around. Then place the frame on a table and arrange cones around both the inner and outer edges, keeping the cones as uniform as possible, smaller ones in the inner circle and larger ones outside. When you know how many cones are needed, cut a ten-inch length of wire for each one. Wind one end of each wire around a cone, near the base, and twist to fasten securely.

When all cones are wired, attach one to the outer edge. Work the cone wire through the frame, from outside to inside, and pull hard, so the base of the cone is firmly seated against the wreath frame. Use pliers to pull wire tight, wind it several times around the inner ring of the wreath frame, then clip off excess wire. Attach several more the same way, pushing the cones close together as you work, then attach one to the inner edge. Work the wire through the frame from inside to outside, pull tight, and fasten wire around the outer ring of the frame between two of the cones already attached. Continue in this way, adding a few outer cones and then one or two inner ones, until both rings are tightly filled.

"Now it's time to do the actual designing of the wreath," Mrs. Horn says. "This is when you need a variety of cones, large and small, some right side up and some upside down. Cut some in two for a different look. Break part of the petals out of some, to get a loose, flowerlike effect."

When she begins the designing, Mrs. Horn works in threes. Attach wires to three large, uniform cones and place them equal distances apart on the central part of the frame—they form a triangle on the circle. Then attach wires near the tips of three or more large cones and attach them, upside down, equal distances between the first three to form a second triangle. The next units added might be half-cones, then cones with part of the petals broken away, then small cones wired together in clusters, but always three at a time, forming triangles. Each time work the cone's wire through the frame, front to back, pull it tight and then wind it several times around a part of the frame.

When the wreath has been loosely filled in this way, begin to add nuts, acorns and buckeyes. Drill a hole through each one, near the base, run one end of a short piece of wire through the hole, and twist to fasten securely. Wire some nuts together in clusters of three. When complete, the nuts and pine cones should be crowded so close together that none can shift.

Lay the completed wreath on newspapers, outdoors, and spray thoroughly with acrylic spray so that all surfaces are coated.

Decorate With Fragrant Herbs

Legend has it that the blossoms of rosemary were white, until the first Christmas. When Mary and Joseph were on their way to Bethlehem they stopped to rest at a place where this fragrant herb grew alongside the road. When Mary rose to go on, the flowers that had been covered by her cloak were blue, like her cloak, and they are blue today.

Our-Lady's-bedstraw gets its name from another legend that says this herb was growing near the stable in Bethlehem and that its sweet-smelling, springy stems were brought in to make a comfortable bed for Mother and Child.

Still another Christmas legend tells how the herb juniper saved the life of the Christ Child when the Holy Family was fleeing from Bethlehem with King Herod's soldiers in hot pursuit. Juniper shrubs bent aside to let Mary, Joseph and the Child pass, and then thrust out their prickly and unruly branches to stop the soldiers.

So use sprigs of rosemary, bedstraw and juniper in your Christmas decorations—the delicate fragrance they bring into the house will be authentically Christmasy!

The word "herb" means any plant that is useful to man, but we usually think of herbs as plants that are scented. Frankincense and myrrh are herbs that grow to tree size.

Over the years many different herbs have been used as medicines, as cleaning aids, for seasoning foods, and for providing pleasant smells to hide unpleasant ones—that was very important in ancient times, when there was never enough soap or hot water to keep things clean.

The sage that flavors the turkey stuffing, the ginger that goes into gingerbread men, cinnamon, peppermint, vanilla—all the things that smell so good in the kitchen at Christmastime—are herbs that grow in one part of the world or another.

Our-Lady's-bedstraw grows along roadsides and in waste places, in many parts of the United States. Rosemary is found in old-fashioned flower gardens, especially in the South. Juniper is a low-growing evergreen planted as an ornamental shrub. Any herb book will teach you how to identify these and many other herbs, and how to start an herb garden where you can grow your own supply of fragrant plants.

People generally harvest their herbs in late summer or fall by cutting the stems, tying them in bunches, and hanging them head down from rafters of garage or attic, where they will give off a pleasant scent while drying. Gather grasses, weeds and some flowers, also, to add variety to your decorations. Old-fashioned strawflowers, coxcomb and baby's breath are good for the purpose. You may also want to save some clusters of berries and seed pods.

Then, when it is time to get ready for Christmas, you can create wreaths or bouquets for each room in the

house, using the herbs for fragrance and the other plant materials for visual accents. You will need only ring-shaped wreath forms, florists' wire, and a supply of the Oasis foam blocks used for flower arranging—all available at craft shops or florists' supply houses.

Since the dry herbs do not need to be in water, a wide variety of containers can be used for bouquets. You can use antique or modern baskets, boxes, or the wooden lugs in which some fruits and vegetables are packed, as well as bowls and vases.

To begin, cut a block of foam to fit down in the bottom of the container you plan to use. If the surface of the block is visible—as in the open box—cover the foam with moss. Place a few large flowers or seed pods first by poking their stems into the foam, then many fine, lacy plant materials around them to fill all the space. If the stems are firm and stiff, no special techniques are needed. If the stems are weak and keep breaking, wrap florists' wire around each stem, to strengthen it, and push the wire end into the foam block.

The box shown is an antique deed case, covered with leather. A stick has been placed at the back, to make sure the lid doesn't come down and smash the plant materials, which include the Christmas herbs plus roadside weeds and strawflowers. Three tiny birds are posed around a nest-shaped arrangement of dry grasses—you can use a real bird's nest in the arrangement if you find one that is neat and attractive. (Collect the nest in autumn, after the birds have left it and before winter winds damage it.)

147

Acknowledgments

Illustrations on pages 14, 15, 30, 31, 43, and 54 reproduced from greeting cards in the collection of The Hallmark Corporation, Kansas City, Missouri.

Illustrations on pages 86 and 87 were painted by Jessie Wilcox Smith for *A Visit From St. Nicholas* by Clement C. Moore. Copyright © 1912 by Houghton Mifflin Company. Reproduced by permission of the publisher.

Songs on pages 132, 134, 136 and 138 arranged by Karl Schulte. Copyright © 1938; copyright renewed 1968 by Western Publishing Company, Inc. Reprinted by permission.

Dried flower arrangements on page 147 by Barbara and Alan White of The Herb Barn, Westfield, Indiana.

TEXT CREDITS

"What Was the Star of Bethlehem?" by Arthur C. Clarke first appeared in *Holiday Magazine*. Copyright © 1954 The Curtis Publishing Company. Reprinted by permission of the author and the author's agents, Scott Meredith Literary Agency, Inc., 845 Third Avenue, New York, N.Y. 10022.

"Susie's Letter From Santa" is from *My Father—Mark Twain* by Clara Clemens. Copyright © 1931 by Clara Clemens Gabrilowitsch renewed 1959 by Clara Clemens Samossoud. Reprinted by permission of Harper & Row, Publishers, Inc.

"Angels" is from *Angels: God's Secret Agents* by Billy Graham. Copyright © 1975 by Billy Graham. Reprinted by permission of the publisher, Doubleday and Company, Inc.

"The Gift of the Magi" is from *The Four Million* by O. Henry. Copyright © 1907 by Doubleday, Page & Company. Reprinted by permission of Doubleday and Company, Inc.

"Winter Wonder" by Donald Culross Peattie first appeared in *Holiday Magazine*. Copyright © 1946 The Curtis Publishing Company. "Gold, Frankincense and Myrrh" by Donald Culross Peattie first appeared in *Good Housekeeping* Magazine. Copyright © 1955 The Hearst Corporation. Both selections reprinted by permission of the author's estate and its agent, James Brown Associates, Inc., 22 East 60th Street, New York, N.Y. 10022.

"Christmas in Brooklyn" is from *A Tree Grows in Brooklyn* by Betty Smith. Copyright © 1943, 1947 by Betty Smith. Reprinted by permission of Harper & Row, Publishers, Inc.

"Conversation About Christmas" by Dylan Thomas. Copyright © 1954 by New Directions Publishing Corporation. Reprinted by permission of New Directions Publishing Corporation.

"Christmas on the Prairie" is from *Little House on the Prairie* by Laura Ingalls Wilder. Text copyright © 1935 by Laura Ingalls Wilder. Copyright renewed 1963 by Roger L. MacBride. Reprinted by permission of Harper & Row, Publishers, Inc.

PICTURE SOURCES

Pages 2,3—The Adoration of the Magi by Fra Lippo Lippi and Fra Angelico. The National Gallery, Washington. Page 7—The Adoration of the Magi by Hieronymus Bosch. The Metropolitan Museum of Art, New York. Kennedy Fund, 1912. Pages 8, 9—The Nativity with Donors and Patron Saints by Gerard David (central panel, detail: angels in upper left). The Metropolitan Museum of Art, New York. Pages 76,77—Brown Brothers, Sterling, Pennsylvania. Page 80—Portrait of Edward VI by Hans Holbein the Younger. The Metropolitan Museum of Art, New York. Collection of Jules S. Bache. Page 88—The Mark Twain Memorial, Hartford, Connecticut. Page 90—Wide World Photos, New York. Page 96, The Theodore Roosevelt Collection, Harvard College Library, Cambridge, Massachusetts.

Illustrations not otherwise credited are from the pages of *The Saturday Evening Post, Country Gentleman*, and *Child Life* magazines, and are the copyrighted property of The Curtis Publishing Company or The Saturday Evening Post Company.